W9-BKE-558

NATIONAL GEOGRAPHIC KIDS

weird but true! 5

NATIONAL GEOGRAPHIC

THAT'S WEIRD!

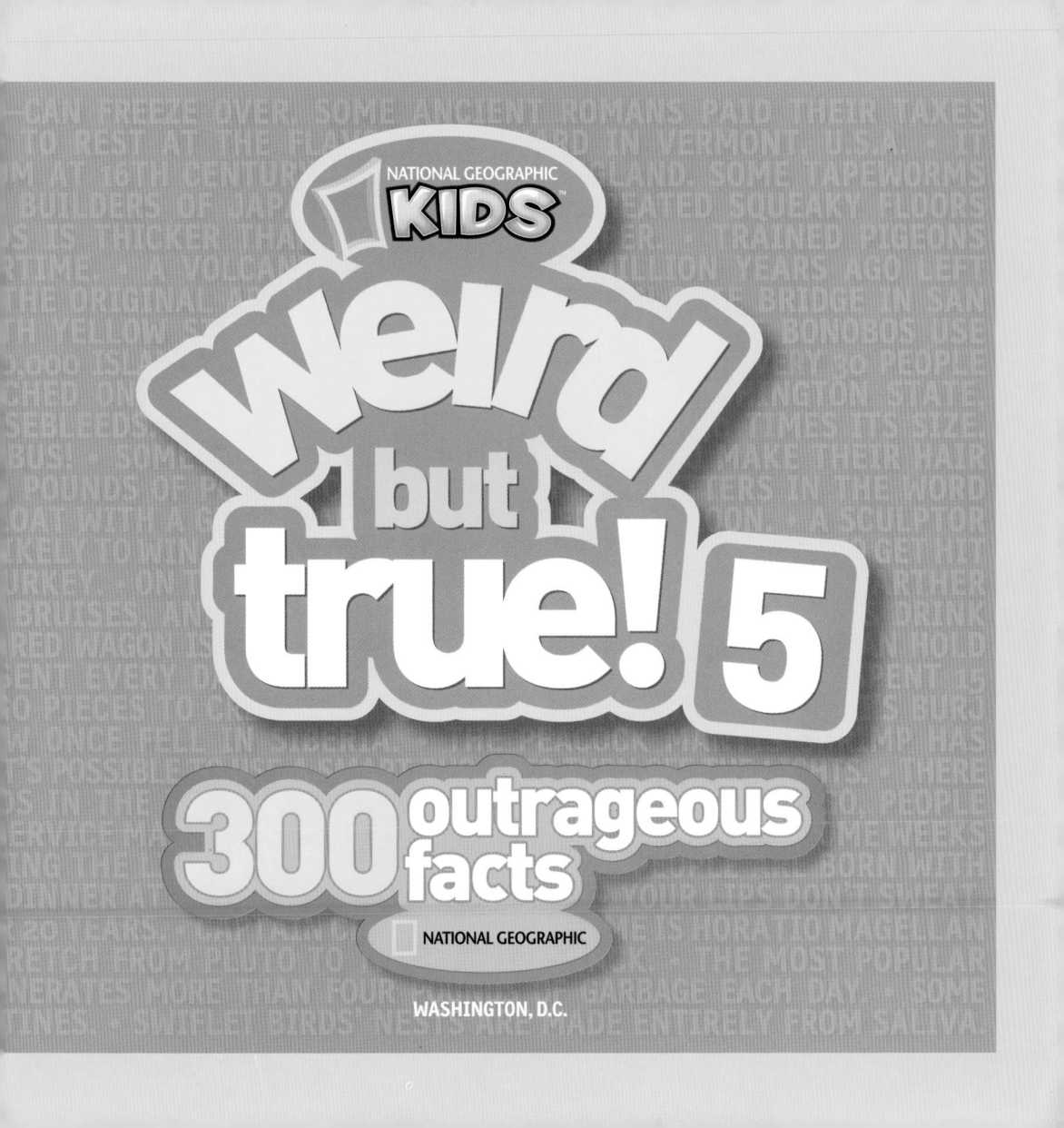
NATIONAL GEOGRAPHIC
KIDS
weird
but
true!
5
300 outrageous facts
NATIONAL GEOGRAPHIC
WASHINGTON, D.C.

Copyright © 2013 National Geographic Society. All rights reserved. Reproduction of the whole or any part of the contents without written permission from the publisher is prohibited.

Visit us online:
Kids: kids.nationalgeographic.com
Parents: nationalgeographic.com/books
Teachers: ngchildrensbooks.org
Librarians: ngchildrensbooks.org

For information about special discounts for bulk purchases, please contact National Geographic Books Special Sales: ngspecsales@ngs.org

For rights or permissions inquiries, please contact National Geographic Books Subsidiary Rights: ngbookrights@ngs.org

Library of Congress Control Number: 2012956100

ISBN (Trade): 978-1-4263-1124-6
ISBN (Library): 978-1-4263-1125-3
ISBN (Scholastic): 978-1-4263-1633-3

Printed in China
13/PPS/2

THAT'S WEIRD!
A T. REX'S ARMS
WERE SO SHORT,
IT COULDN'T
SCRATCH ITS NOSE!

The world's biggest skateboard is almost as long as a school bus!

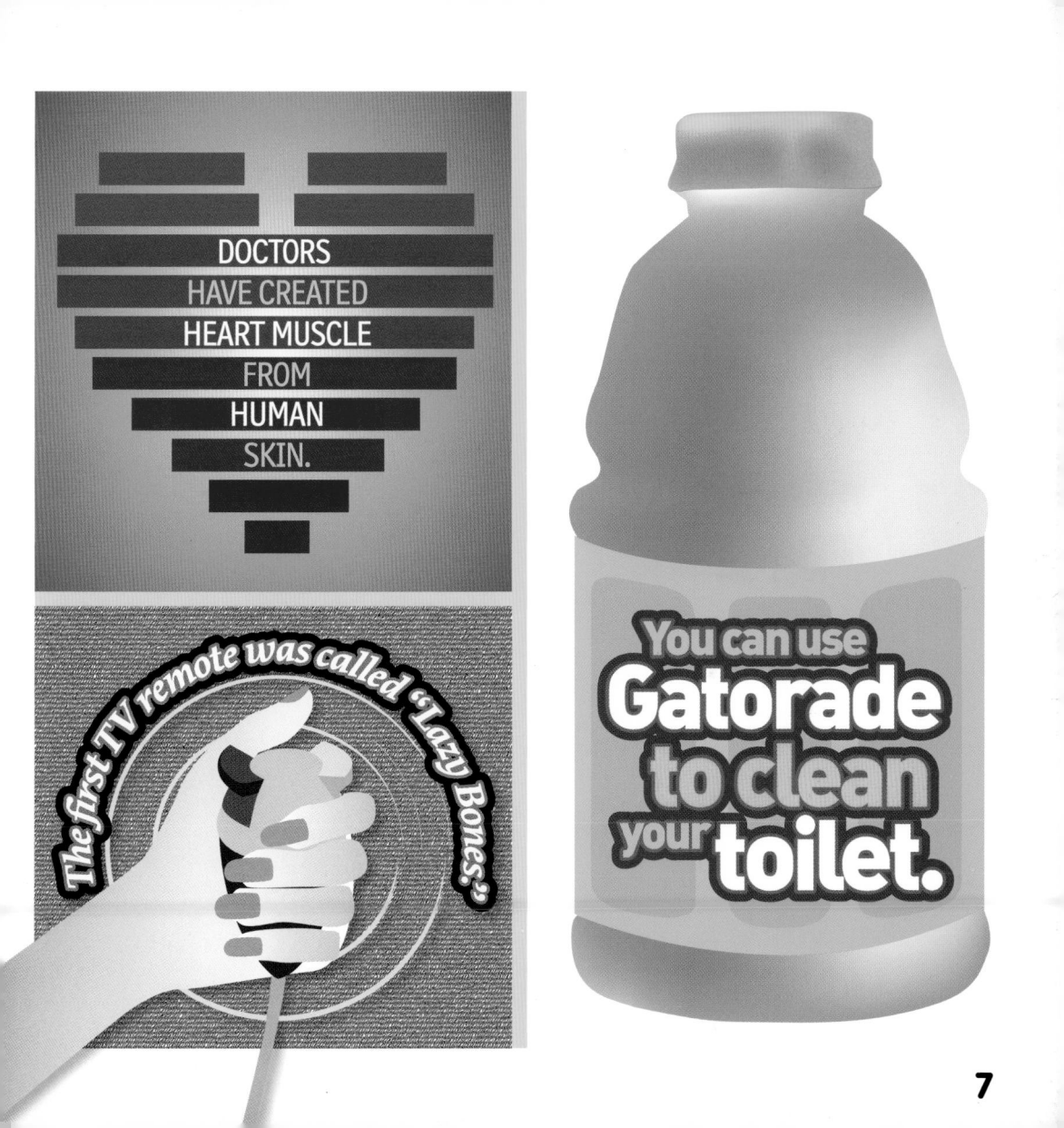
DOCTORS
HAVE CREATED
HEART MUSCLE
FROM
HUMAN
SKIN.
The first TV remote was called "Lazy Bones."
You can use
Gatorade
to clean
your toilet.

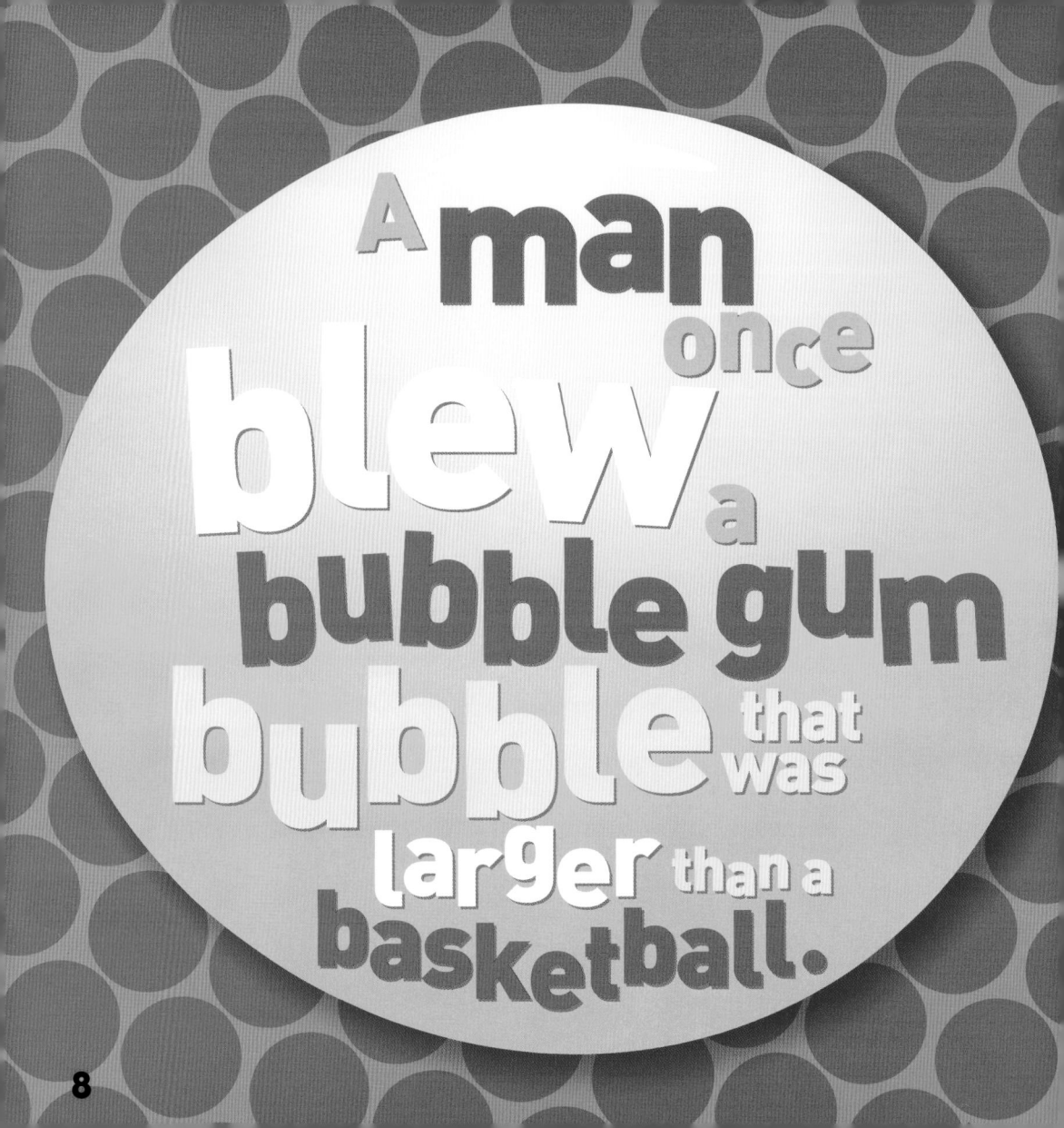
A man once blew a bubble gum bubble that was larger than a basketball.

There's more salt in one gallon of (3.79 L) sea water than in 49 pounds (22.3 kg) of potato chips!

A GROUP OF HIPPOS IS SOMETIMES CALLED A **BLOAT.**

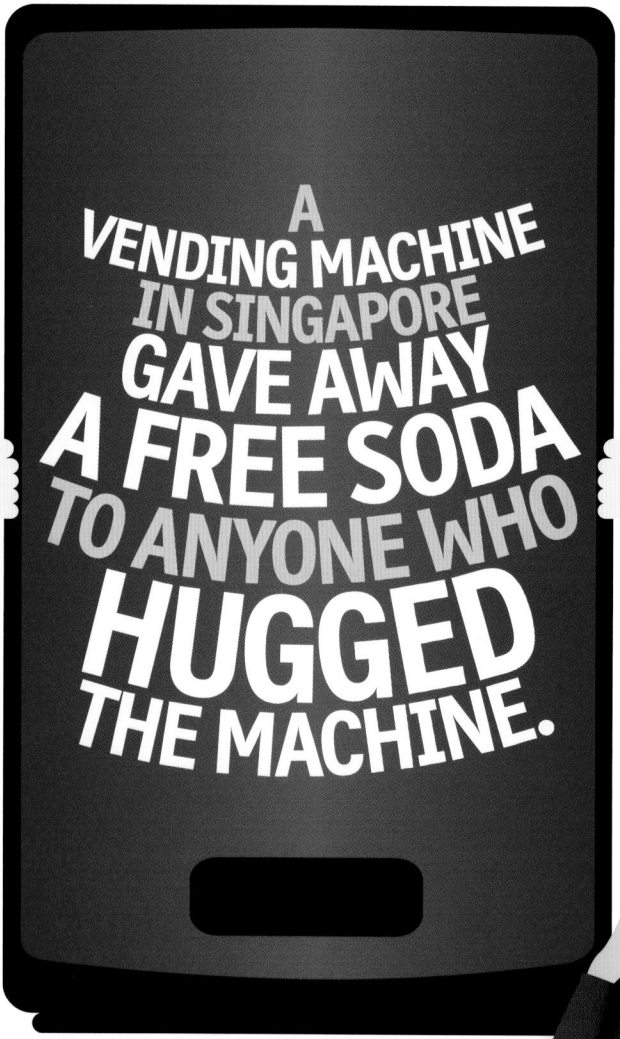
A
VENDING MACHINE
IN SINGAPORE
GAVE AWAY
A FREE SODA
TO ANYONE WHO
HUGGED
THE MACHINE.

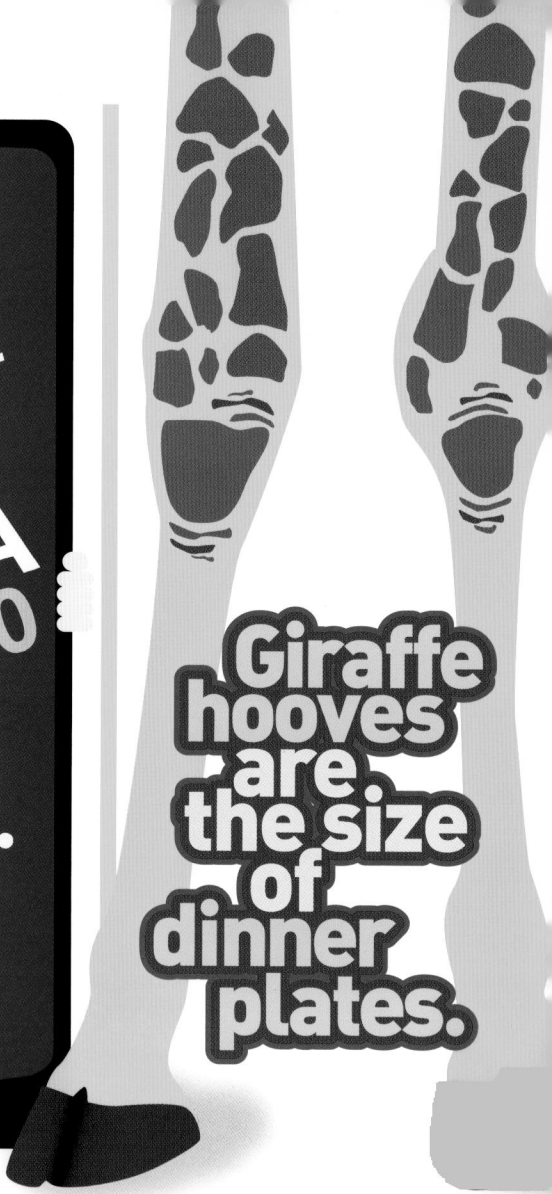
Giraffe hooves are the size of dinner plates.

ALL OF THE LETTERS IN THE WORD "TYPEWRITER"

CAN BE FOUND IN ONE ROW ON A KEYBOARD.

HOT WATER CAN FREEZE FASTER THAN COLD WATER.

Sea snail mucus was once used to make purple dye.

The first cars didn't have windshield wipers.

CLOCKS WERE ONCE MADE WITH ONLY ONE HAND.
XII
I
II
III
IV
V
VI
VII
VIII
IX
X
XI

SHARKS CAN'T BLINK.

A GERMAN **FASHION** DESIGNER MAKES **CLOTHING** FROM **MILK POWDER.**

GOATS SNACK ON POISON IVY.

Ostriches can **swim** but they can't fly.

A U.S. ice-cream shop sold insect-flavored ice cream.

TRAINED PIGEONS HAVE DELIVERED SECRET MESSAGES ACROSS ENEMY LINES DURING WARTIME.

Sticking raw bacon in your nostrils can stop serious nosebleeds.

MALE TURKEYS ARE CALLED GOBBLERS.

BEES HAVE FIVE EYES.

SOME BLUEBERRIES ARE PINK.

THERE ARE
180,000 ISLANDS
IN FINLAND—
THAT'S ONE FOR ABOUT
EVERY 30 PEOPLE
IN THE COUNTRY.

Some
crabs
are bright purple.

SOME
ANTS
LICK
EACH
OTHER
TO PROTECT
AGAINST
DISEASES.

SOME **POLICE OFFICERS** IN CAIRO, EGYPT, PATROL THE **PYRAMIDS** ON **CAMELBACK.**

Spider silk is used to make fishing nets in some countries.

Raindrops
are shaped
like
hamburger
buns.

Hello Kitty EVA AIR

A Taiwanese airline flies Hello Kitty–themed jets.

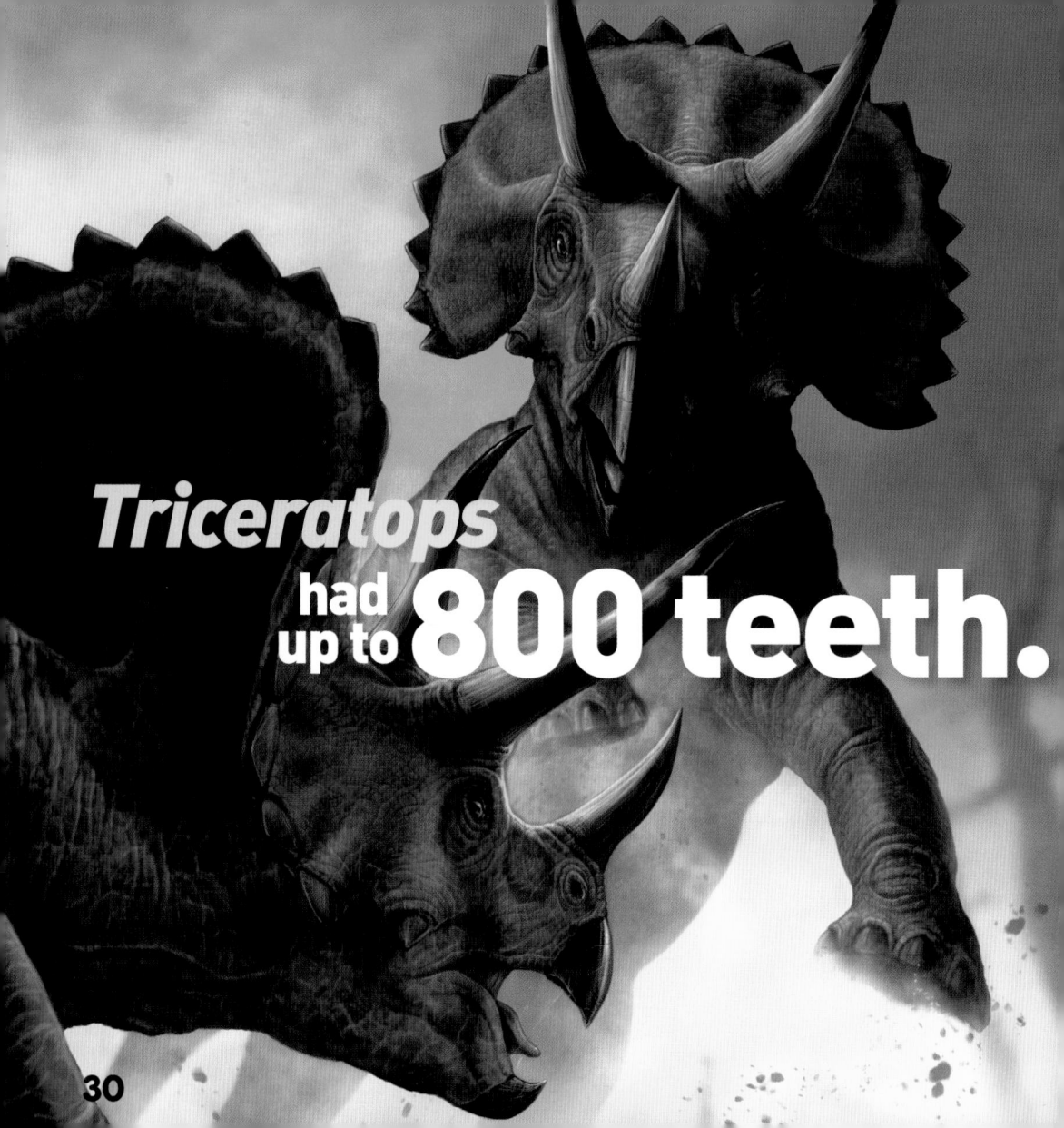

Triceratops had up to **800 teeth.**

WHEN IT GETS COLD ENOUGH,
NIAGARA FALLS—
ONE OF THE
LARGEST WATERFALLS
IN NORTH AMERICA—
CAN FREEZE OVER.

A CANADIAN WOMAN

RODE A MOTORIZED TOILET UP TO 46 MILES AN HOUR!

(74 kph)

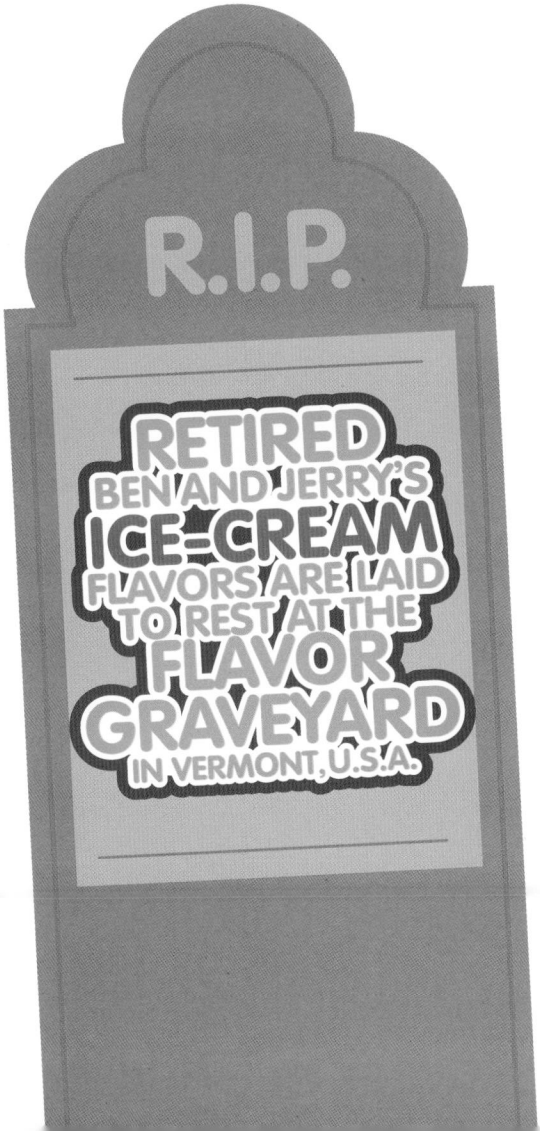

Insect blood can be clear, yellow, or green.

IT CAN BE MORE SATISFYING TO SCRATCH AN ITCH ON YOUR BACK THAN ON YOUR ARM.

A 35-FOOT-TALL, (10.7 m) INFLATED ANGRY BIRD PERCHED ON THE SIDE OF THE SEATTLE SPACE NEEDLE, IN WASHINGTON STATE, U.S.A.

Kinkajous can twist their hind feet **backward** to climb trees.

YOU WOULD WEIGH
ZERO POUNDS
AT THE CENTER OF THE (0 kg)
EARTH.

A Welshman's dog served as best man at his wedding.

IF YOUR TONGUE WAS AS LONG AS A FROG'S, IT WOULD REACH DOWN TO YOUR BELLY BUTTON!

VAMPIRE BATS ARE THE ONLY MAMMALS TO HAVE A BLOOD-ONLY DIET.

A candy company makes gummy bears the size of footballs.

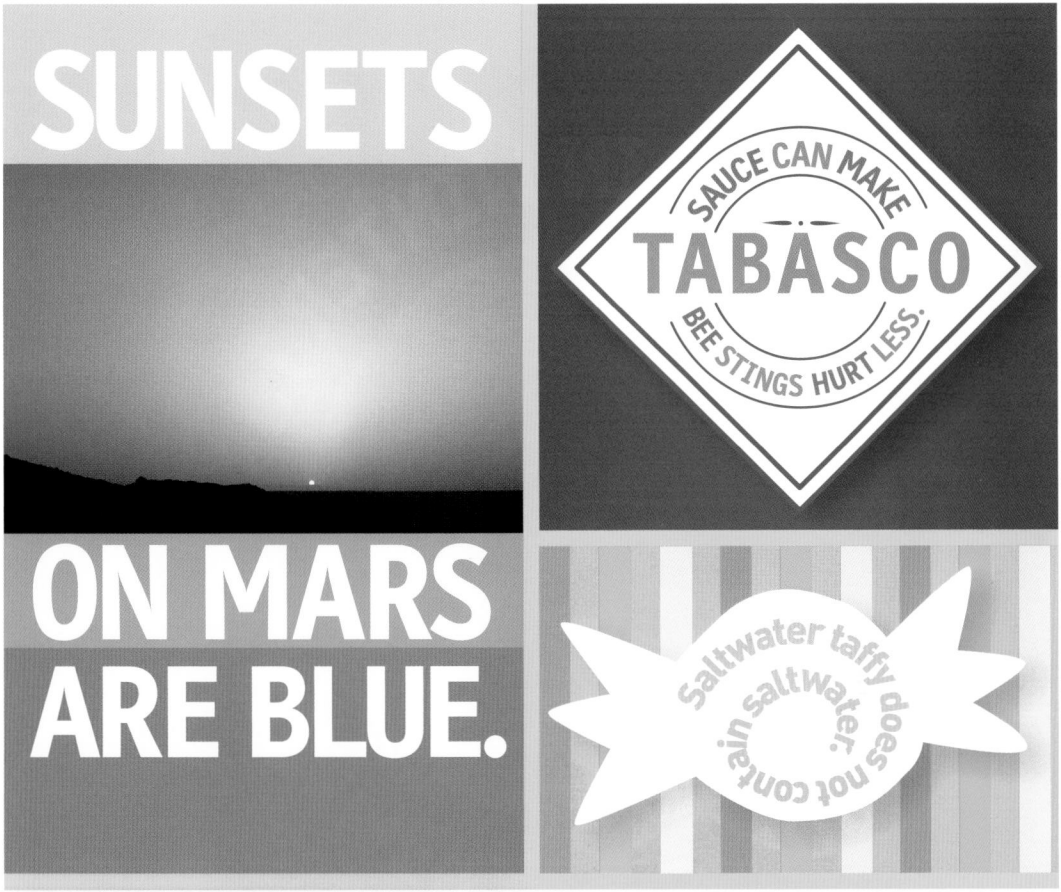

THERE'S A MILLIPEDE THAT HAS 750 LEGS.

FULL MOONS APPEAR BRIGHTER IN WINTER THAN IN SUMMER.

MORE PEOPLE HAVE BEEN TO
THE MOON
THAN TO THE BOTTOM OF THE OCEAN.

SOME BONOBOS USE TOUCH-SCREEN COMPUTERS TO COMMUNICATE WITH HUMANS.

Turtles the size of small cars roamed Earth 60 million years ago.

A leech can suck up five times its body weight in **blood.**

Thermal vents—cracks in the ocean floor—spew water that's hotter than 750°F (400°C)

Ping-Pong balls can travel (113 kph) ***70 miles an hour—*** *that's faster than a speeding car!*

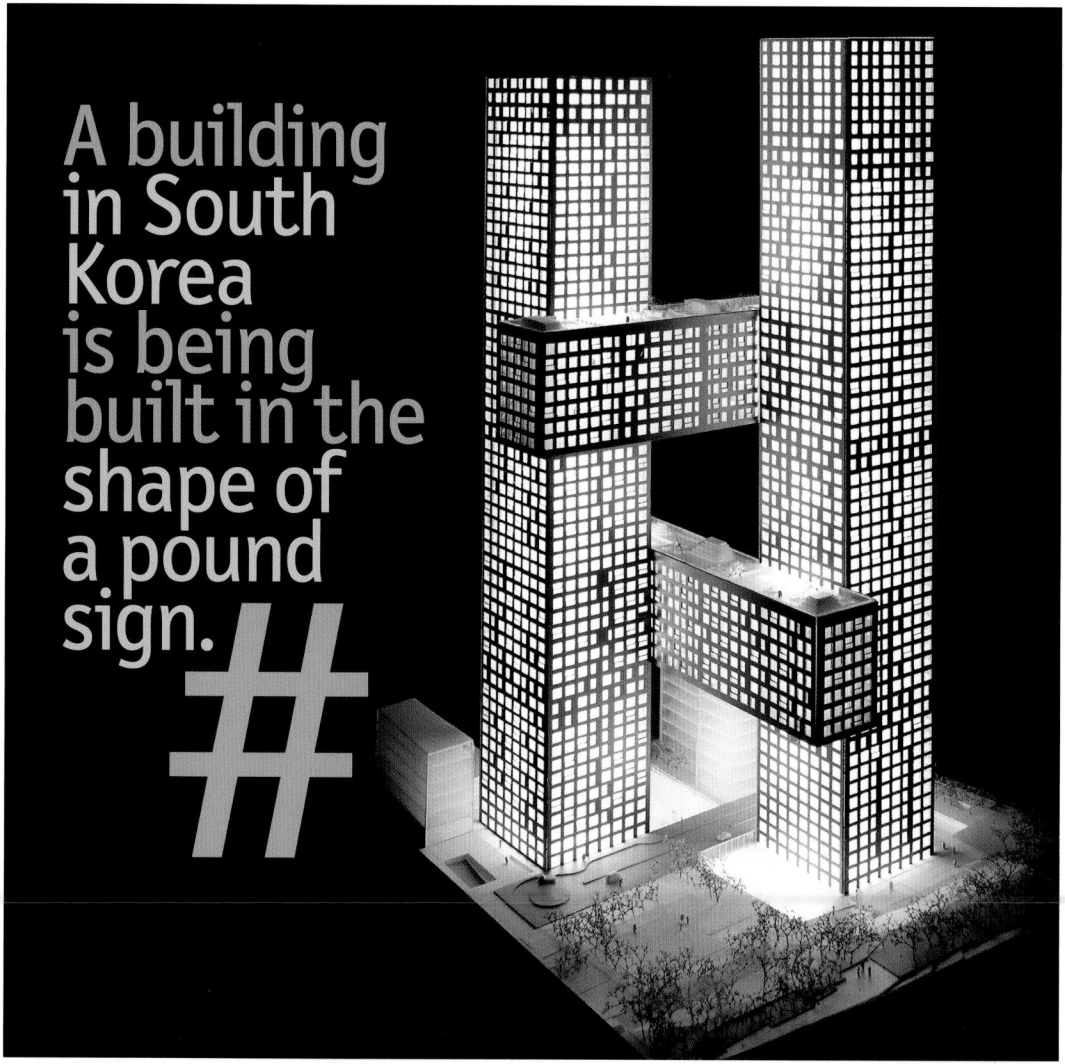
A building in South Korea is being built in the shape of a pound sign.
#

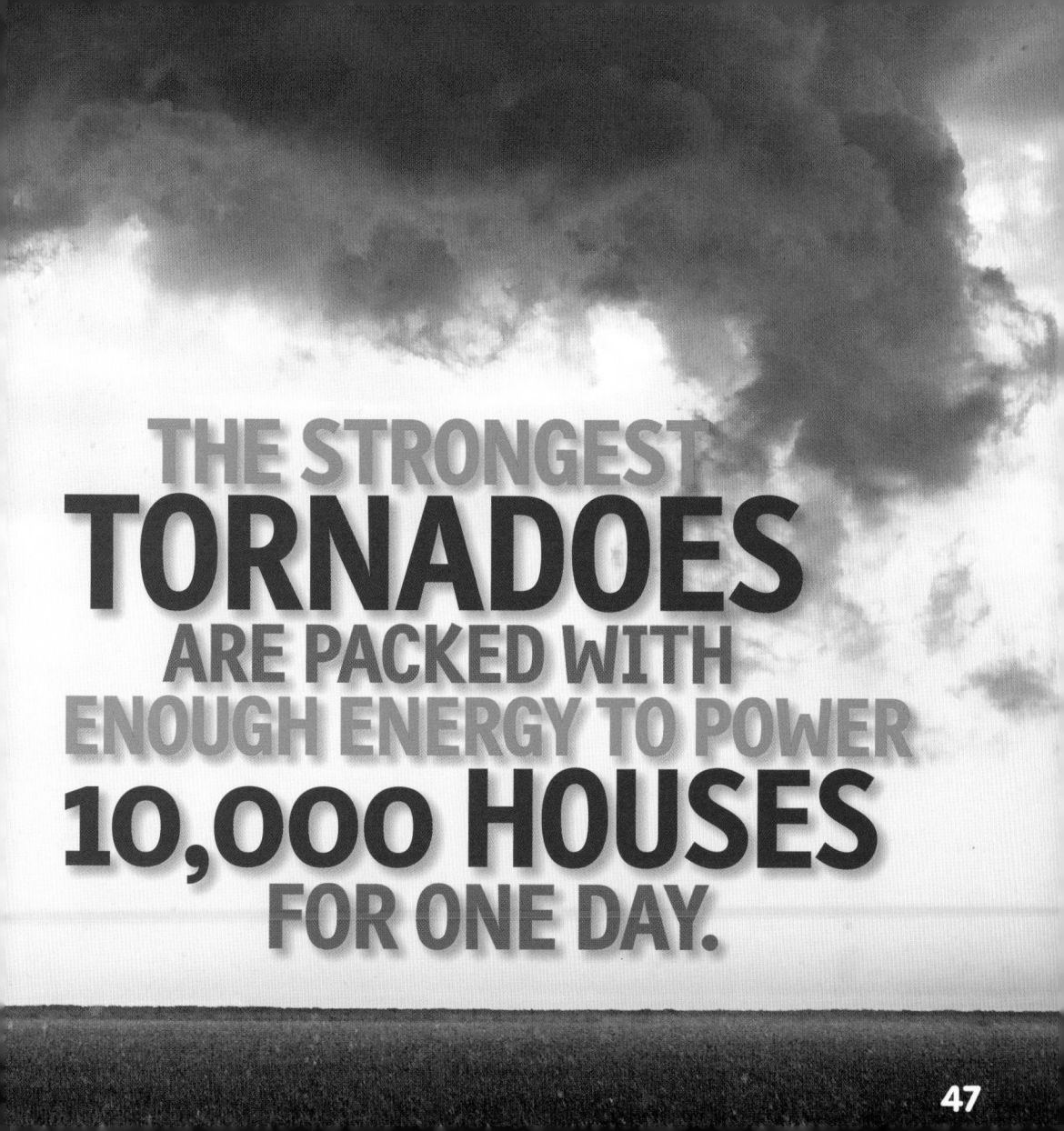
THE STRONGEST
TORNADOES
ARE PACKED WITH
ENOUGH ENERGY TO POWER
10,000 HOUSES
FOR ONE DAY.

A WHITE ORCA WAS SPOTTED IN THE PACIFIC OCEAN.

SOME TARANTULAS ARE BLUE.

You can
buy a wig
for your dog.

BUILDERS OF JAPAN'S NIJO CASTLE CREATED SQUEAKY FLOORS TO PREVENT INTRUDERS FROM SNEAKING IN.

A sea star can turn its stomach inside out.

A baseball stadium in Texas, U.S.A., sold hot dogs that were each longer than two iPads.

ALLIGATOR TEETH

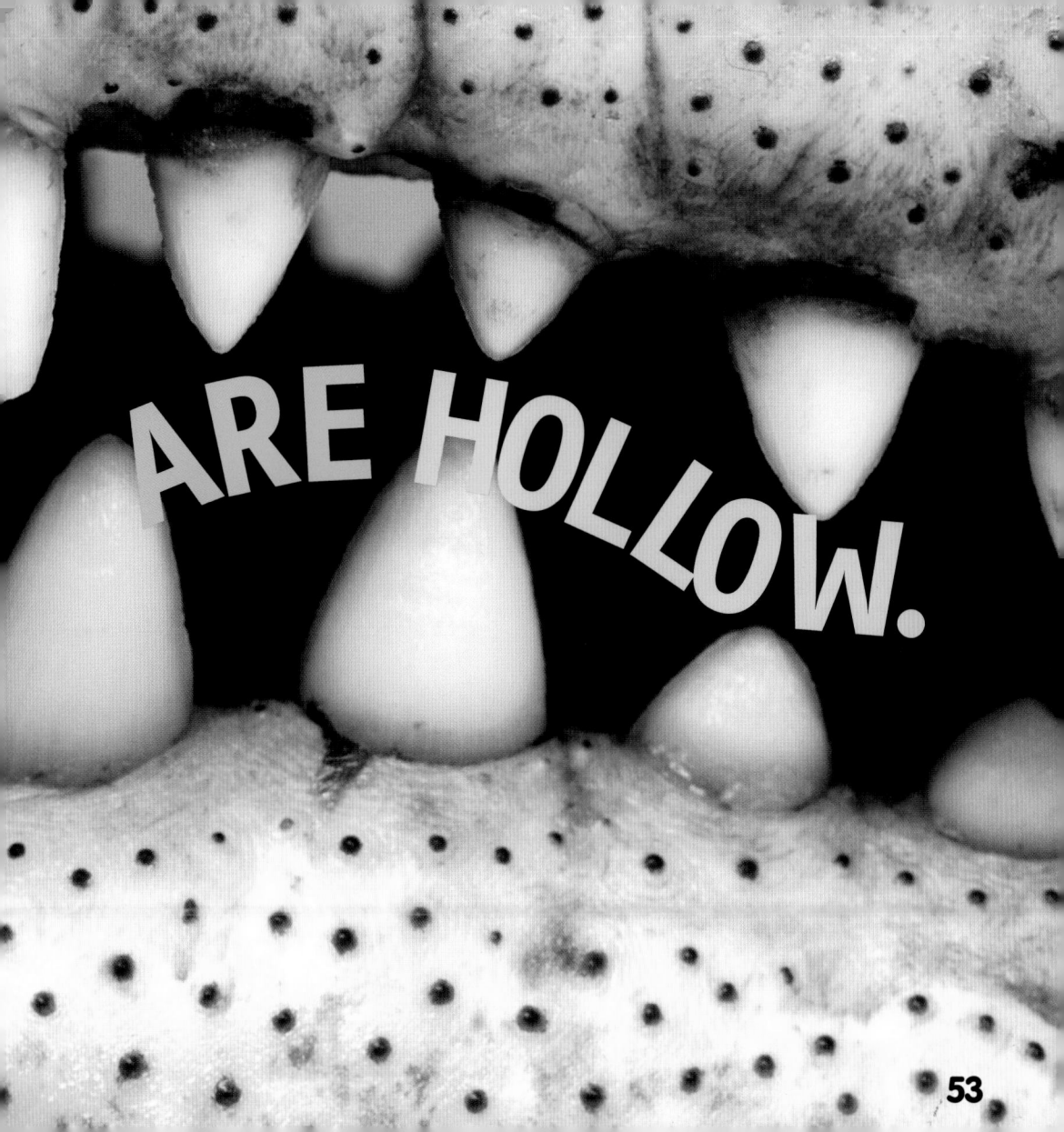
ARE HOLLOW.

THE WORLD'S LARGEST BAT HAS A WINGSPAN AS WIDE AS A SOFA.

FINGERPRINTS
CAN LAST FOR
UP TO
40 YEARS
ON
PAPER.

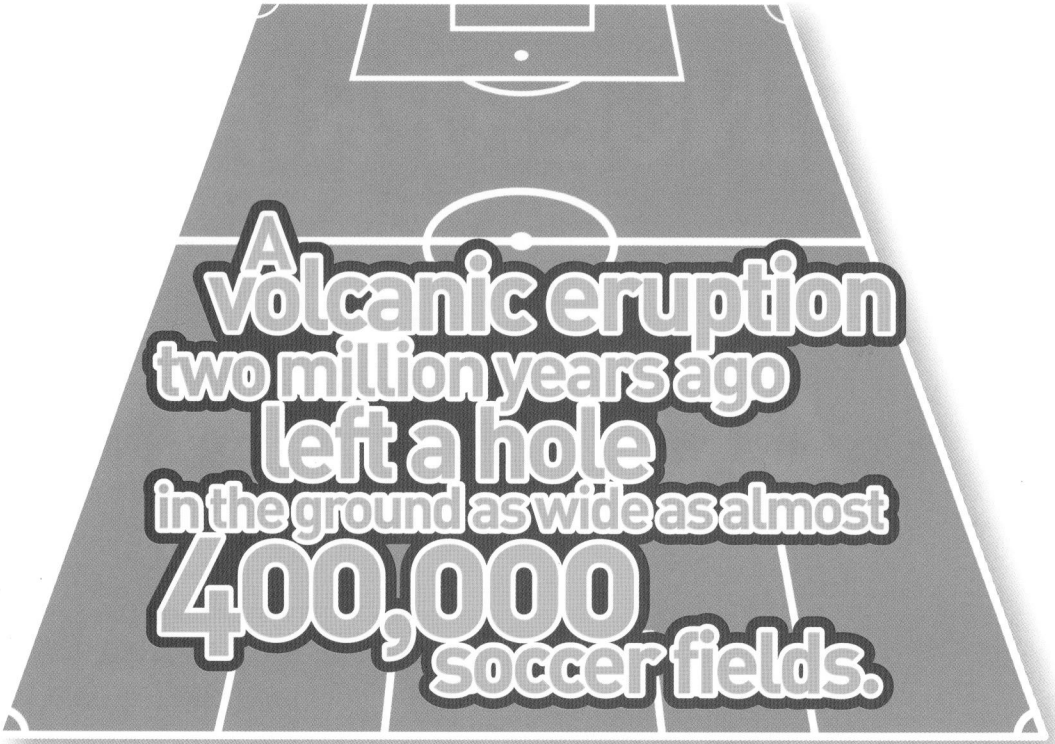

YOU COULD COOK A **LARGE PIZZA** ON THE SURFACE OF **VENUS** IN **NINE SECONDS!**

Ladybugs might play dead when threatened.

Babies have taste buds in their cheeks.

Spaceship Earth
at Walt Disney
World Resort in
Florida, U.S.A.,
weighs as much as
17 jumbo
jets.

Whales have belly buttons.

A prize
cow
in Canada
sold for
1.2 million
dollars.

A STUDY FOUND THAT THE **MORE AFRAID** YOU ARE OF **SPIDERS,** THE **BIGGER** THEY APPEAR TO BE.

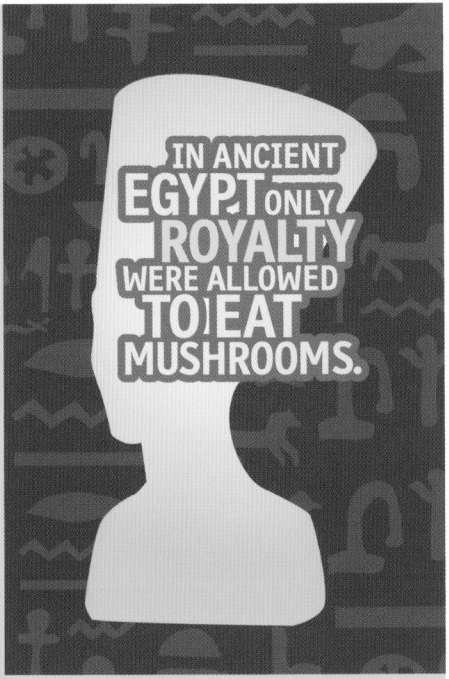

Some people are born with a double row of eyelashes.

Young giraffes sometimes moo.

12,345,678,

$$\begin{array}{r} 111{,}111{,}111 \\ \times\, 111{,}111{,}111 \\ \hline 987{,}654{,}321 \end{array}$$

Some ancient Romans paid their taxes in honey.

It was considered good luck to throw shoes at the bride and groom at 16th-century weddings in England.

A hot drink can sometimes cool you down faster than a cold drink.

BEAVERS HAVE A SET OF CLEAR EYELIDS TO SEE UNDERWATER.

UP UNTIL 100 YEARS AGO, SOME TOOTHBRUSH BRISTLES WERE MADE FROM PIG HAIRS.

SEAWEED CAN PREVENT TOOTH DECAY.

Fish sometimes cough.

OOLOGY
IS THE STUDY OF
BIRD
EGGS.

There's a jellyfish that can change from an adult back into a baby.

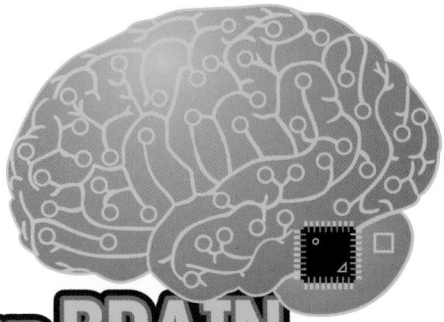

YOUR BRAIN CAN HOLD 100 TIMES MORE INFORMATION THAN A COMPUTER.

THE ORIGINAL ARCHITECTS OF THE
GOLDEN GATE BRIDGE
IN SAN FRANCISCO, CALIFORNIA, U.S.A.,
CONSIDERED PAINTING THE BRIDGE
BLACK WITH
YELLOW STRIPES
INSTEAD OF
ORANGE.

A MAN IN HAVANA, CUBA, BUILT A BICYCLE THAT'S AS TALL AS AN ELEPHANT!

Cockroaches recognize members of their family.

400 million tweets are sent every day.

There's a town in Oregon named Boring.

A PARADE FLOAT
WITH A GIANT
BALLOON
IS CALLED A
FALLOON.

IT TOOK

450,300 LEGO BRICKS

TO CREATE AN

18-FOOT-TALL (5.5 m)

REPLICA OF

THE WORLD'S TALLEST BUILDING!

ASTRA

IS THE FEAR OF

PHOBIA

THUNDER AND LIGHTNING.

A chameleon's tongue can travel as fast as 13 miles (21 kph) an hour.

An insect called an **assassin bug** sometimes carries **dead ants** on its back to appear **bigger.**

Only female mosquitoes bite.

Whale blubber was once used to make margarine.

THE WORLD'S LARGEST RED WAGON IS TALLER THAN A

TWO-STORY BUILDING AND CAN HOLD 75 KIDS.

CAMELS ARE ORIGINALLY FROM NORTH AMERICA.

AMERICANS ARE MORE LIKELY TO WIN A MILLION DOLLARS IN THE LOTTERY THAN TO GET HIT BY LIGHTNING.
9 23 9 8 18 11

BABY EELS ARE CALLED
ELVERS.

ON THE MOON YOU CAN THROW A BALL SIX TIMES FARTHER THAN YOU CAN ON EARTH.

An octopus can detach an arm on purpose and then regrow it.
The symbol &, which means "and," was once a letter in the English alphabet.
You can buy an energy bar with crickets inside.

YOU CAN SEE A **GLASS FROG'S HEART** BEATING THROUGH ITS SKIN.

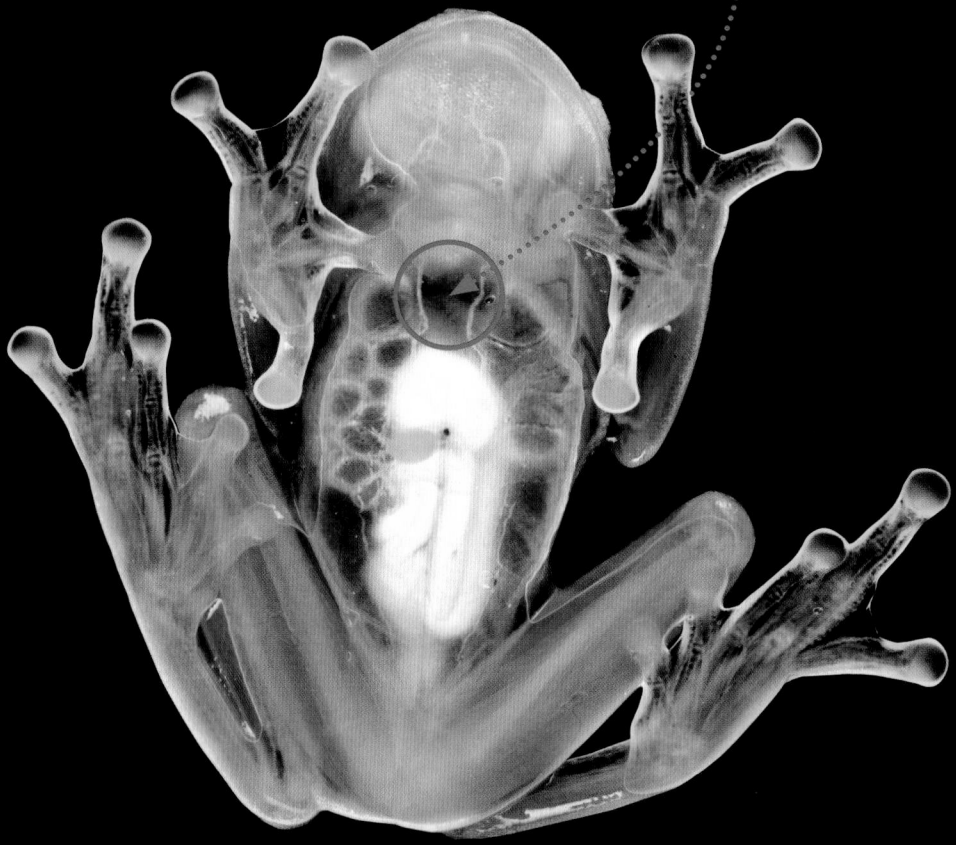

You will likely get

10,000

small cuts,

bruises,

and

sprains

in your lifetime.

A BUZZ LIGHTYEAR ACTION FIGURE SPENT 15 MONTHS ON THE INTERNATIONAL SPACE STATION.

THAT'S WEIRD!

An elephant's
heart
can weigh as
much as a
basset hound.

A LION'S
ROAR
IS LOUDER
THAN A LAWN
MOWER.

AGGRESSOR

YOU CAN TELL THE PERSONALITY OF SOME FINCHES BY THE COLOR OF THEIR HEADS—BIRDS WITH BLACK HEADS ARE RISK-TAKERS WHILE REDHEADS ARE MORE AGGRESSIVE.

RISK-TAKER

In Japan you can buy octopus-flavored ice cream.

Orange snow once fell in Siberia.

Some millipedes glow in the dark.

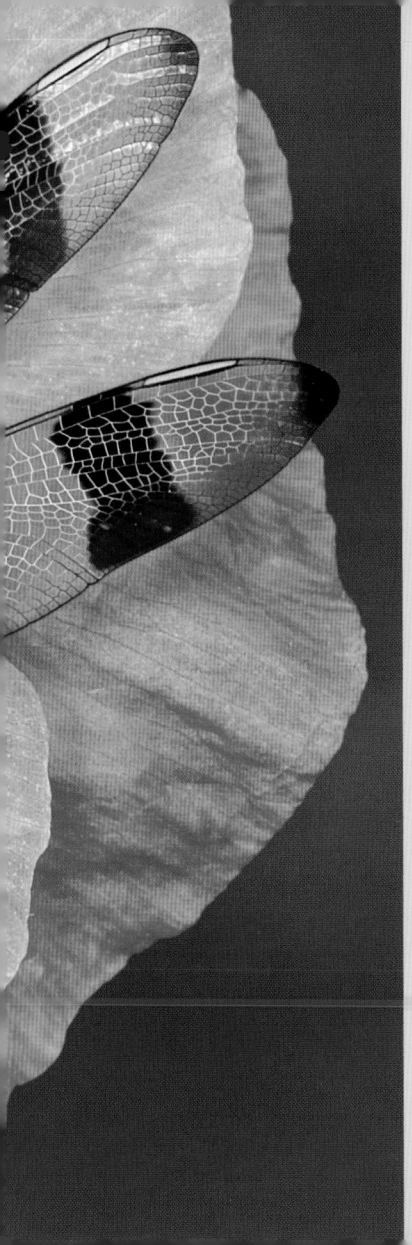

300 MILLION YEARS AGO, DRAGONFLIES HAD WINGSPANS AS WIDE AS THREE FRISBEES.

Children in ANCIENT ROME played a game similar to LEAPFROG.

COLLEGE STUDENTS CREATED A PIANO OUT OF bananas.

EVERY DAY THERE ARE MORE **iPHONES SOLD** AROUND THE WORLD THAN THERE ARE **BABIES BORN.**

THE **PEACOCK MANTIS SHRIMP** HAS CLAWS STRONG ENOUGH TO **PUNCH** THROUGH AN AQUARIUM'S GLASS WALLS.

Doodling
can help
you
concentrate

MORE THAN 100 YEARS AGO, PEOPLE ROLLER-SKATED

BY STRAPPING SMALL TIRES TO THEIR FEET.

THERE ARE MORE **TORTOISES** THAN PEOPLE ON **SEYCHELLES,** A GROUP OF ISLANDS IN THE INDIAN OCEAN.

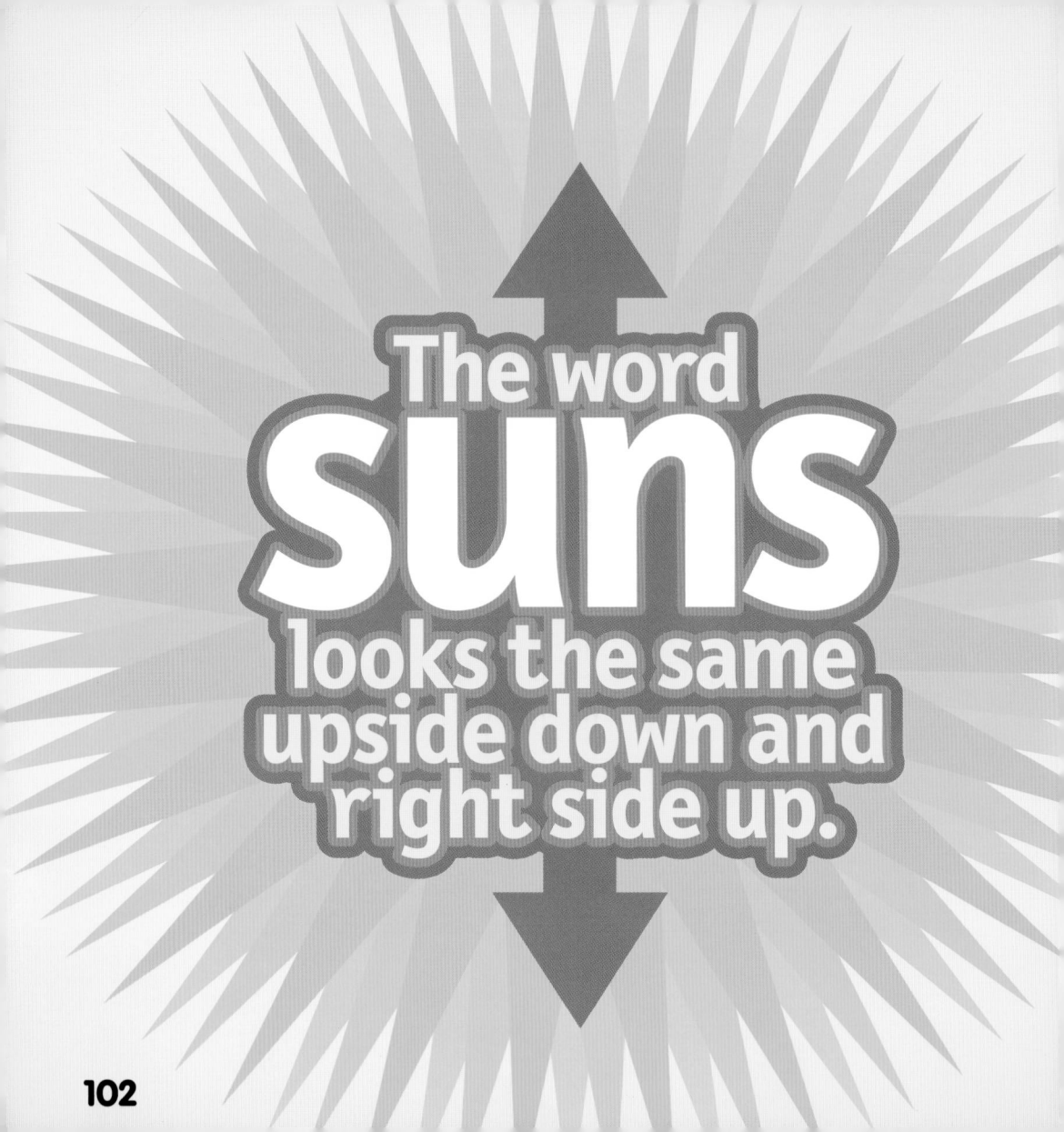
The word
suns
looks the same
upside down and
right side up.

It's possible to use a smart-phone to turn off the lights.

Soup made from birds' nests is a Chinese delicacy.

A TURKISH MAN CAN SQUIRT MILK OUT OF HIS EYE, SHOOTING THE LIQUID OVER NINE FEET. (2.795 m)

LEGEND SAYS THAT PIRATE TREASURE MAY BE BURIED NEAR THE STATUE OF LIBERTY.

YOU CAN ORDER FRIED BONE MARROW FOR DINNER AT SOME FANCY RESTAURANTS.

THE U.S. POSTAL SERVICE MAILS MORE THAN 800,000 LIVE CHICKENS IN THE WEEKS LEADING UP TO EASTER.

Chili pepper crops grow hotter when there is less rain.

IT'S POSSIBLE FOR
A CROCODILE
TO EAT A SHARK.

SOME SPIDERS' BRAINS EXTEND INTO THEIR LEGS.

BEAGLE

BOXER

BOGLE

THE INSIDE OF A CUCUMBER CAN BE UP TO 20 DEGREES F COOLER (11.1°C) THAN THE OUTSIDE AIR.
Your lips don't sweat.
CRACKERS ARE NAMED FOR THE CRACKLING SOUND THEY MAKE WHILE BAKING.
THE MWANZA flat-headed agama lizard resembles SPIDER-MAN.

One type of Australian orchid spends its entire life underground.

YOU CAN BUY A

$25,000 DOGHOUSE

THAT COMES WITH

AIR-CONDITIONING AND A MUSIC SYSTEM!

NIGHTTIME RAINBOWS ARE COMMON AT YOSEMITE NATIONAL PARK

IN CALIFORNIA, U.S.A.

MOST TORNADOES OCCUR BETWEEN 3 p.m. AND 9 p.m.

A meteor crater in South Africa is wider than Ireland.

IT TOOK ABOUT 2.6 MILLION PEOPLE TO BUILD

JAPAN'S TODAIJI TEMPLE IN THE EIGHTH CENTURY A.D.

A platypus **swims** with its ears and nostrils shut.

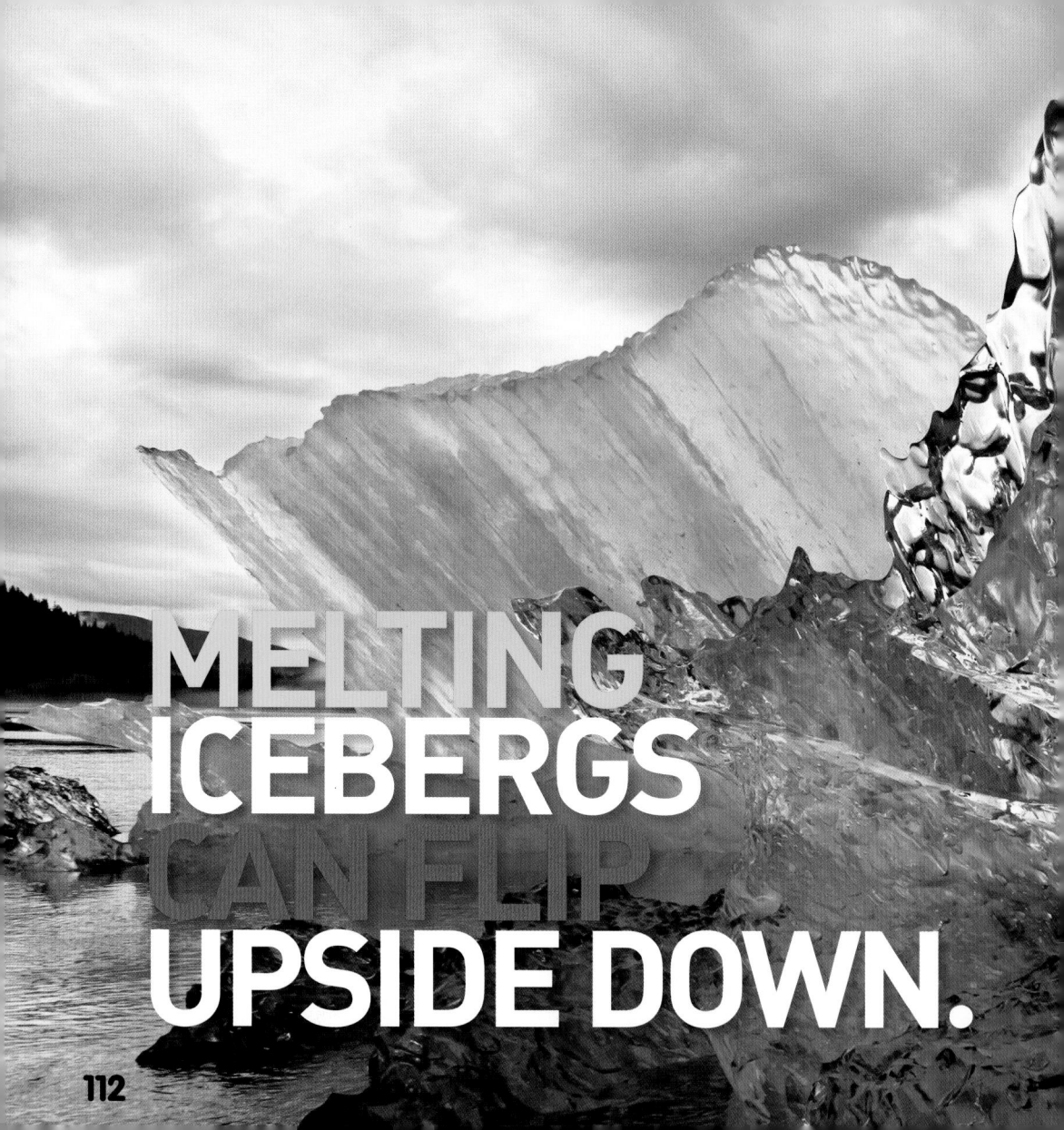

MELTING ICEBERGS CAN FLIP UPSIDE DOWN.

Fireflies can glow yellow, green, or orange.

A BOARD GAME WAS FOUND IN KING TUT'S TOMB.

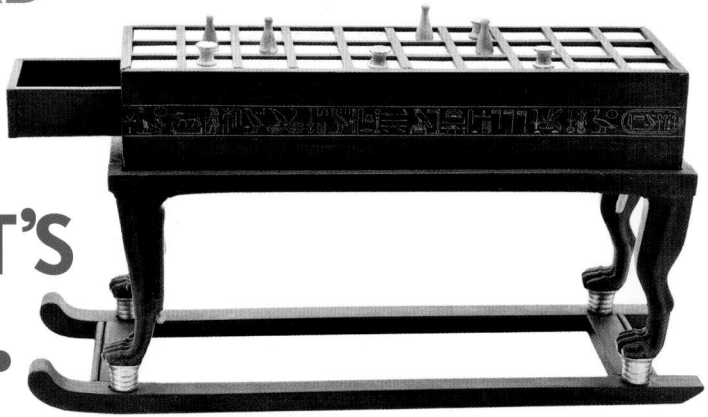

TUBEWORMS CAN LIVE FOR ABOUT **600 YEARS IN THE DEEP OCEAN.**

THE AUSTRALIAN **LYREBIRD** CAN MIMIC **CAR ALARMS.**

One million
pieces of
sporting
equipment
were used during the
2012 Olympic Games.

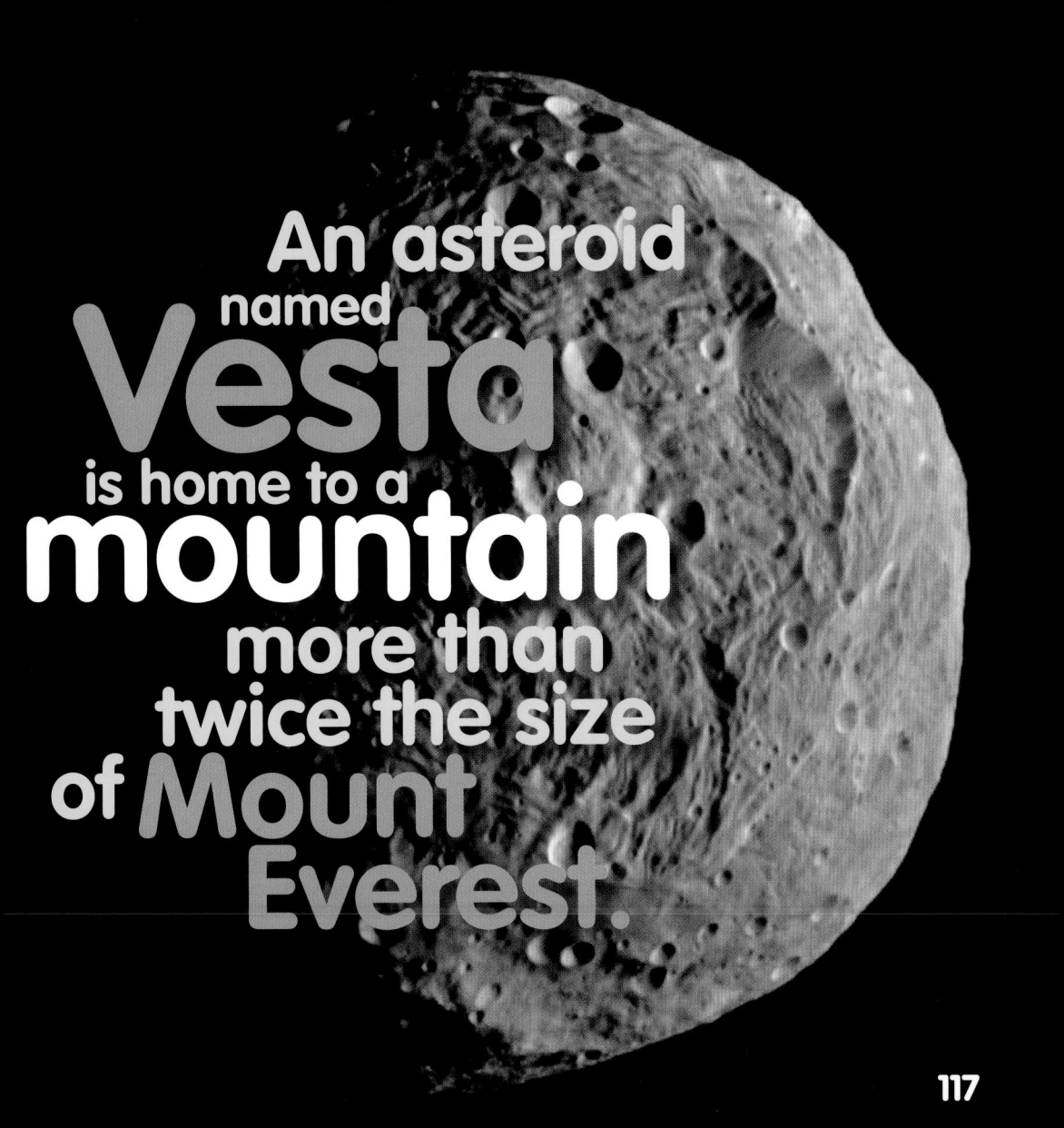
An asteroid
named
Vesta
is home to a
mountain
more than
twice the size
of Mount
Everest.

BILLIONS OF YEARS AGO, EARTH REACHED 3,700°F. (2,038°C) THAT'S SEVEN TIMES HOTTER THAN A BARBECUE GRILL AT A COOKOUT.

A GERMAN MAN DROVE ONE CAR 500,000 MILES (804,672 km) IN 23 YEARS.

THAT'S THE SAME DISTANCE AS DRIVING AROUND THE GLOBE 20 TIMES.

(287 million metric tons)

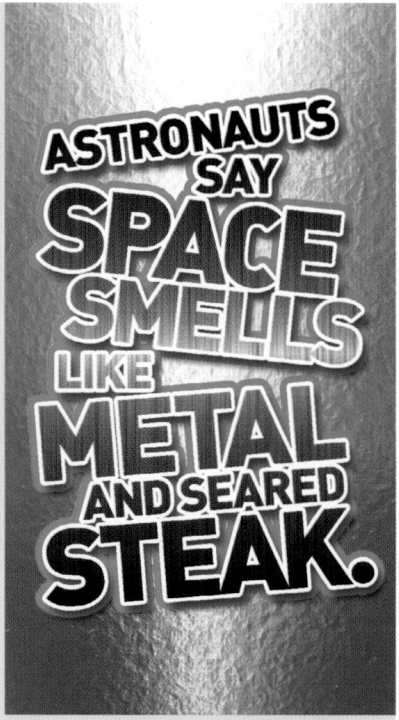

PREHISTORIC SNAKES, CALLED TITANOBOAS, GREW AS LONG AS SCHOOL BUSES.

RHINO HORNS ARE MADE OF THE SAME SUBSTANCE AS HUMAN FINGERNAILS.

IT'S CONSIDERED RUDE TO WRITE IN RED INK IN PORTUGAL.

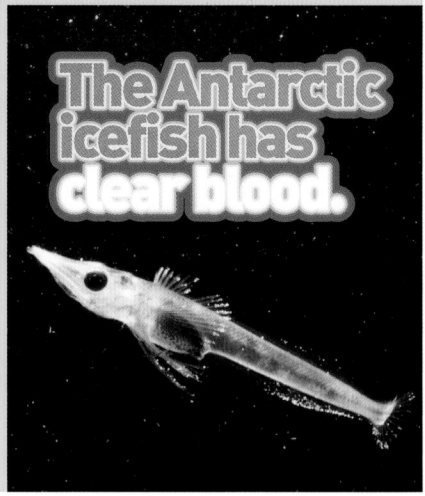

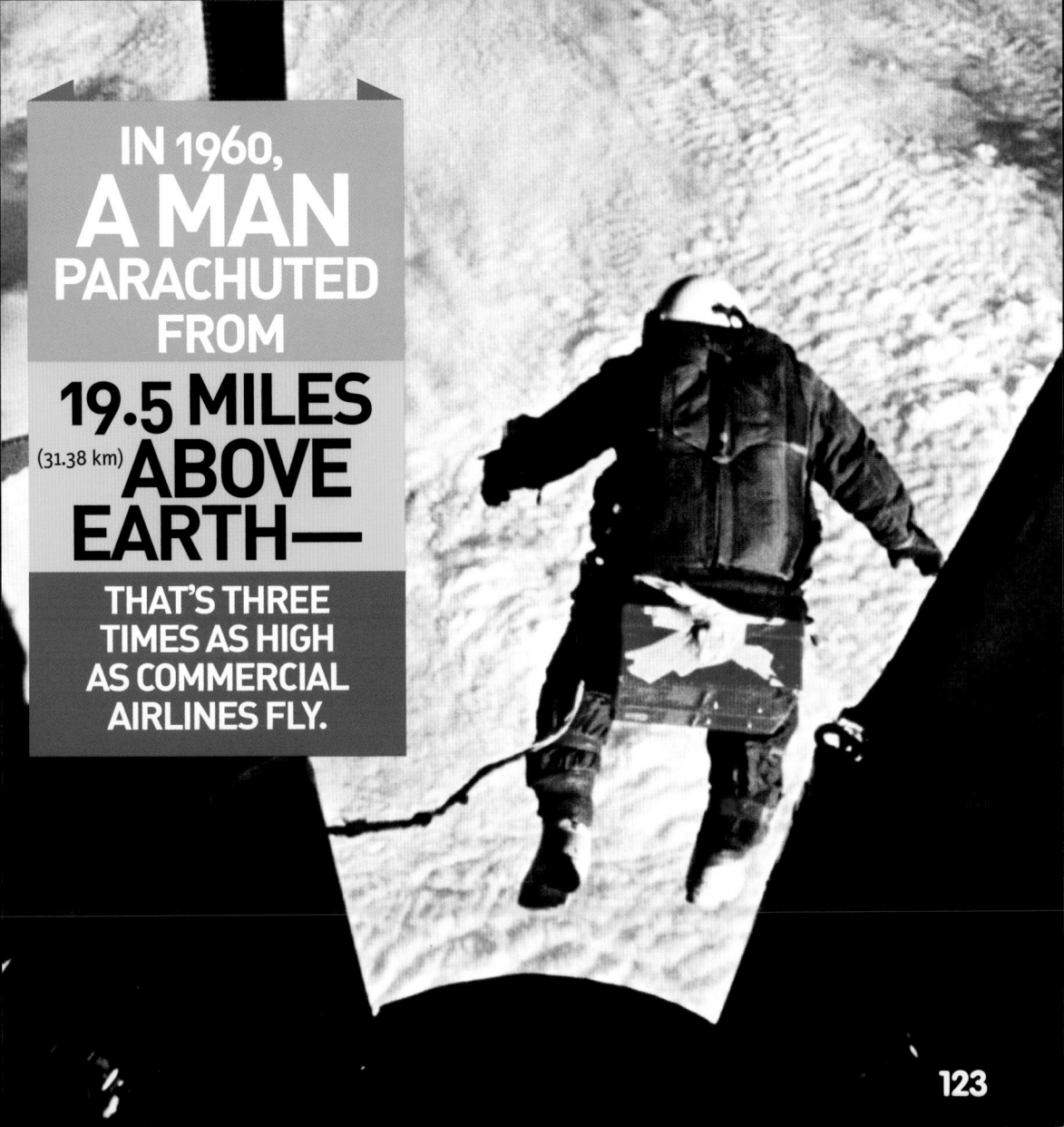

IN 1960, A MAN PARACHUTED FROM 19.5 MILES (31.38 km) ABOVE EARTH—

THAT'S THREE TIMES AS HIGH AS COMMERCIAL AIRLINES FLY.

A LEMUR CAN WEIGH AS LITTLE AS FIVE QUARTERS OR AS MUCH AS A CAR TIRE, DEPENDING ON THE SPECIES.

THAT'S WEIRD!

CANADA PRODUCED ENOUGH MAPLE SYRUP IN ONE YEAR TO FILL 13 OLYMPIC-SIZE POOLS.

SOME WALLABIES HAVE LIGHT PURPLE FUR.

A SALTWATER CROCODILE MAY KEEP ITS MOUTH OPEN TO HELP ITS BRAIN STAY COOL.

There is a **sneaker** with built-in **screens** that display Twitter messages.

IT TAKES **65 TONS** (59 metric tons) OF PAINT TO COVER THE EIFFEL TOWER.

IN THAILAND, PEOPLE HAVE **WATER FIGHTS** TO CELEBRATE NEW YEAR'S.

THE FLAP OF
SKIN UNDER A
MOOSE'S
THROAT
IS CALLED
A BELL.

There was no ice in Antarctica 55 million years ago.

IN SINGAPORE, PEOPLE WERE ONCE FINED FOR NOT FLUSHING PUBLIC TOILETS.

THE RHINOCEROS BEETLE CAN LIFT 850 TIMES ITS BODY WEIGHT.

Ancient Maya warriors hurled containers full of hornets at enemies.

THE BODY WEIGHT OF A **SUNFISH** INCREASES

60 MILLION TIMES IN ITS LIFETIME.

(AT THAT RATE, A HUMAN WOULD GROW TO WEIGH AS MUCH AS FOUR *TITANIC* CRUISE SHIPS!)

A KOMODO DRAGON CAN SWALLOW A GOAT WHOLE.

There's a
90 percent
chance your
parents
will steal
some of your
Halloween
candy.

SCIENTISTS HAVE RETRIEVED

800,000-YEAR-OLD ICE FROM A GLACIER IN ANTARCTICA.

A POPULAR SOFT DRINK IN THE UNITED KINGDOM IS MADE WITH DANDELIONS.

SOME
BAOBAB
TREES
IN AFRICA
ARE MORE THAN
2,000
YEARS OLD.

ATLANTIC
HERRING
SOMETIMES
FORM SCHOOLS
THE SIZE OF
NEW YORK CITY.

YOU CAN FIND MORE THAN
1,000 ANCIENT DINOSAUR
AND REPTILE FOOTPRINTS ALONG THE
"DINOSAUR FREEWAY"—
STRETCHING FROM COLORADO TO NEW MEXICO, U.S.A.

A half-inch-long (1.3 cm) flatworm has 60 eyes.

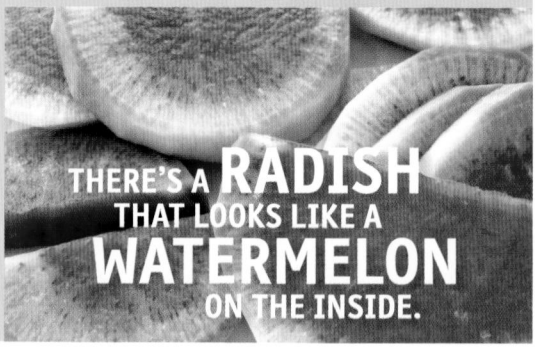

A GUENON MONKEY'S
WARNING CALL SOUNDS
LIKE A LOUD SNEEZE.

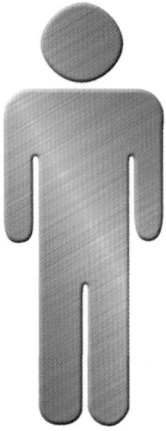

THE HUMAN BODY CONTAINS A TINY AMOUNT OF GOLD.

A home run in baseball is also called a "tater."

DETROIT RED WINGS HOCKEY FANS SOMETIMES THROW DEAD OCTOPUSES ONTO THE ICE RINK TO CELEBRATE A WIN.

THE EARTH ONCE SPUN 0.1 MILLISECONDS FASTER EACH DAY FOR TWO WEEKS.

A REINDEER'S
NOSE
HEATS UP
AIR
ON THE WAY
TO THE
LUNGS.

AN 18-HOLE
GOLF COURSE
LIES BETWEEN
TWO RUNWAYS
AT AN AIRPORT
IN ASIA.

ROASTED
ANTS
ARE A POPULAR
SNACK
IN COLOMBIA.

PEOPLE CREATE **HUMAN TOWERS** UP TO **THREE STORIES TALL** AT FESTIVALS IN SPAIN.

LA VANGUARDIA
aturem el CI
LA VANGUARDIA

When you're driving on the highway, the car engine is hot enough to cook a piece of chicken.

There's an annual beauty pageant for camels in the United Arab Emirates, a country in Asia.

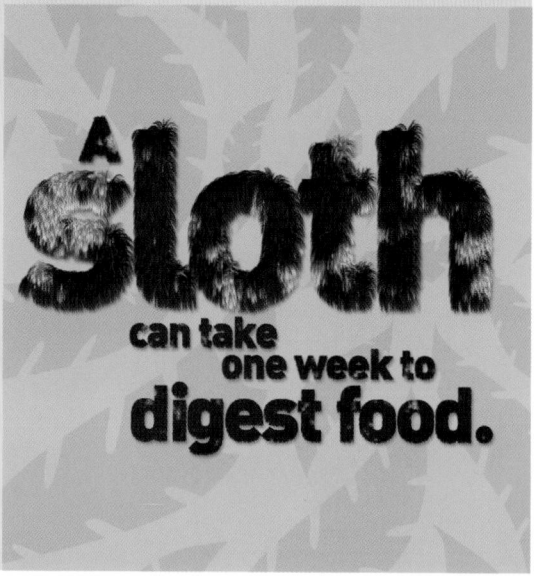
A sloth can take one week to digest food.

The number 4 is considered unlucky in China.
A 25,000-YEAR-OLD FOOTPRINT WAS FOUND IN A FRENCH CAVE.
Strawberries are members of the rose family.

A TYPICAL AMERICAN GROCERY STORE
IS STOCKED WITH ABOUT
50,000 ITEMS.

Yawns are more contagious among family members than among strangers.

Some 70 million years ago, a rodentlike creature the size of a rabbit was the largest mammal on Earth.

Elephant seals
can stay underwater
for up to two hours.

IT'S TRADITION FOR NASA ENGINEERS TO EAT PEANUTS FOR GOOD LUCK DURING SPACE MISSIONS.

THE AVERAGE HOME PRODUCES MORE AIR POLLUTION THAN A CAR.

There are about 14 million fake Facebook accounts.

A STUDY FOUND THAT THE SOUND OF A KNIFE SCRAPING A BOTTLE IS ONE OF THE MOST UNPLEASANT SOUNDS IN THE WORLD.

AN ALBATROSS CAN GLIDE THOUSANDS OF MILES WITHOUT FLAPPING ITS WINGS.
(kilometers)

YOU CAN WATCH
A MOVIE IN A
GRAVEYARD
AT THE CINESPIA THEATER
IN CALIFORNIA, U.S.A.

Production of Hershey's Kisses was halted during World War II because the foil used to wrap them was rationed.

In Bulgaria and Greece, nodding your head up and down means "no."

A WOODPECKER PECKS A TREE AT 15 MILES (24 kph) AN HOUR.

DOGS HAVE
THREE
TIMES
MORE

TASTE
BUDS
THAN CATS.

IT'S POSSIBLE FOR YOU TO SPOT THE LIGHT OF A CANDLE FROM 14 MILES AWAY.
YOUR BRAIN REMEMBERS 10,000 SCENTS.
CHILDREN'S HEARING IS MORE SENSITIVE THAN ADULTS'.

YOUR BODY CAN DETECT TASTE IN JUST .0015 SECONDS— THAT'S AS FAST AS A BLINK OF AN EYE.
YOUR STOMACH CAN EXPAND TO 40 TIMES ITS SIZE.
THE SKIN ON YOUR HANDS IS THICKER THAN 15 SHEETS OF PAPER.
YOU HAVE ABOUT 17,000 TOUCH RECEPTORS IN EACH OF YOUR HANDS.

BUBBLEGUM CORAL IS BRIGHT PINK AND CAN GROW TALLER THAN A TWO-STORY BUILDING.

PEOPLE LIVING ON PENTECOST ISLAND IN THE SOUTH PACIFIC HAVE BEEN USING VINES TO BUNGEE JUMP FOR 1,500 YEARS.

BLUE-RINGED OCTOPUSES CAN POISON HUMANS.

Alpaca moms **hum** to comfort their babies.

Swiflet birds' nests are made entirely from saliva.

Canned tuna is one of the most popular pizza toppings in Germany.

Gelada **monkey** calls sound like a person saying "yep, yep, yep."

THERE'S A PLACE IN VENEZUELA, SOUTH AMERICA, WHERE **LIGHTNING** FLASHES UP TO **280 TIMES** AN HOUR.

FLAMINGOS DON'T TURN PINK UNTIL THEY ARE ABOUT TWO YEARS OLD.

The Mississippi River sometimes flows backward during powerful hurricanes.

The iPod's name was inspired by this line from the classic movie 2001: A Space Odyssey: "Open the pod bay doors."

SNAKES DO NOT HAVE EYELIDS.

THERE'S A BEACH IN HAWAII WITH GREEN SAND.

SOME TAPEWORMS CAN GROW TO BE 40 FEET LONG (12 m) INSIDE HUMAN INTESTINES.

Some 75,000 pounds of meat sank (34,019 kg) on the R.M.S. *Titanic*.

Yak hair was used to make wigs for characters in The Hobbit movie.
HALF OF THE PIGS IN THE WORLD LIVE IN CHINA.

A MALL IN THE DESERT CITY OF DUBAI, UNITED ARAB EMIRATES, **MAKES SNOW** FOR AN INDOOR SKI RESORT.

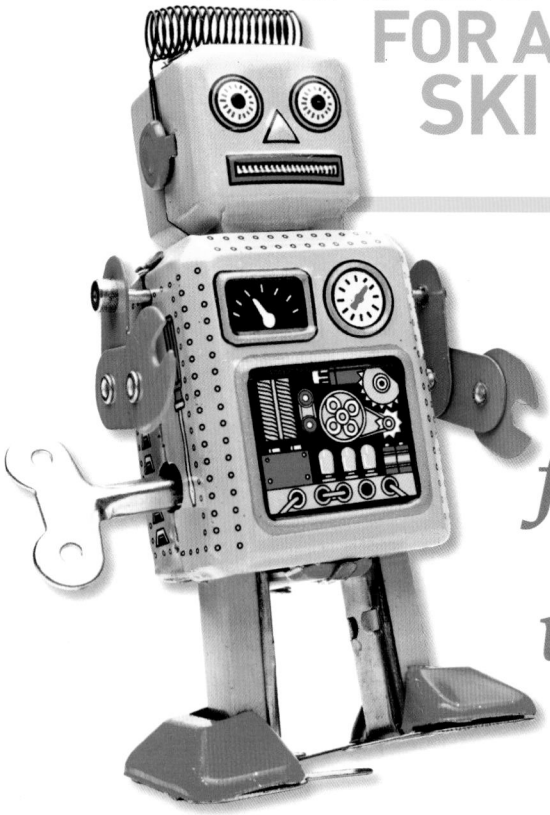

The word "robot" first appeared in a play written in 1929.

THE AVERAGE ADULT TELLS ABOUT 11 LIES IN A WEEK.

There's a forest of
crooked trees
in Poland.

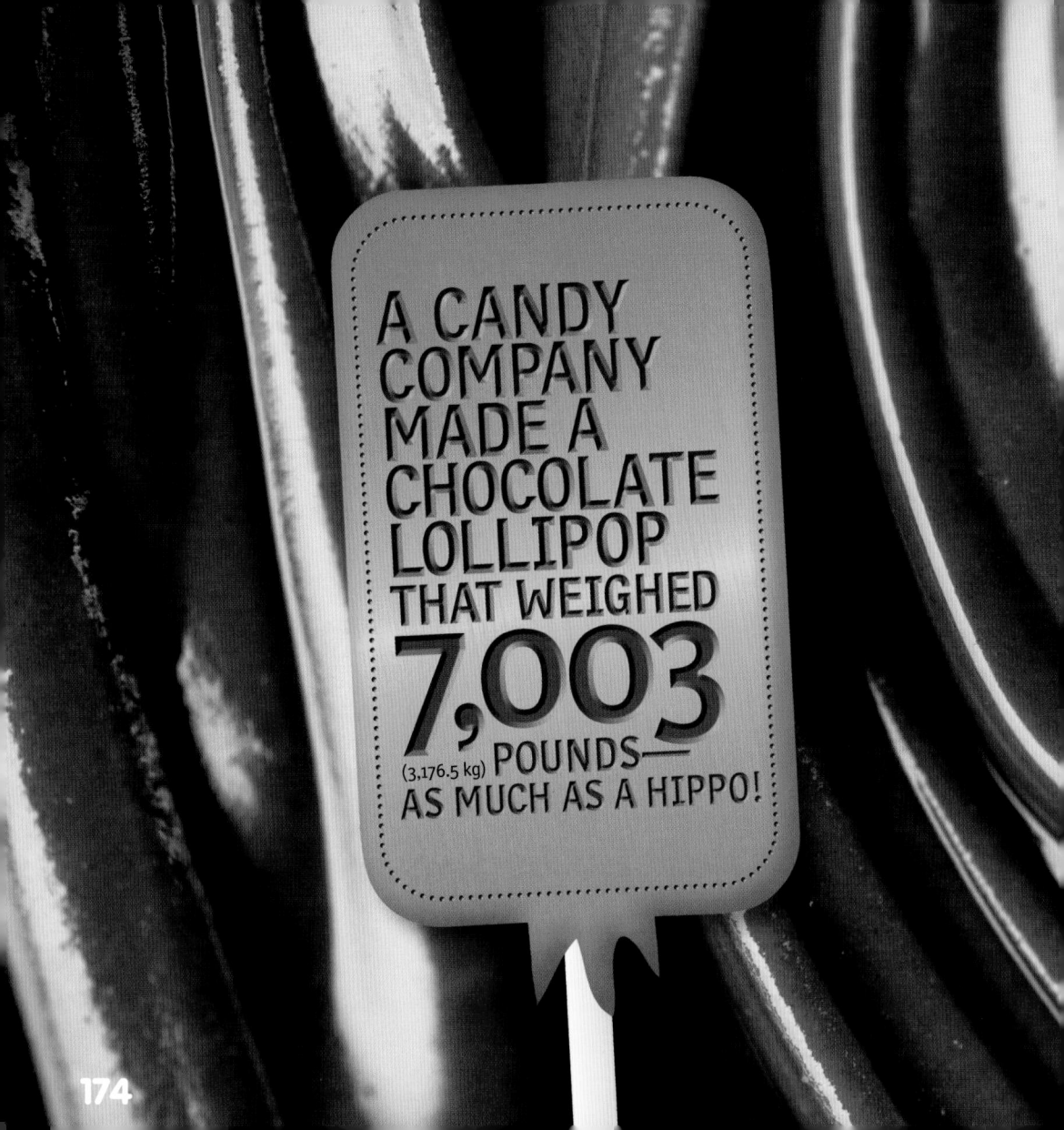
A CANDY COMPANY MADE A CHOCOLATE LOLLIPOP THAT WEIGHED 7,003 (3,176.5 kg) POUNDS—AS MUCH AS A HIPPO!

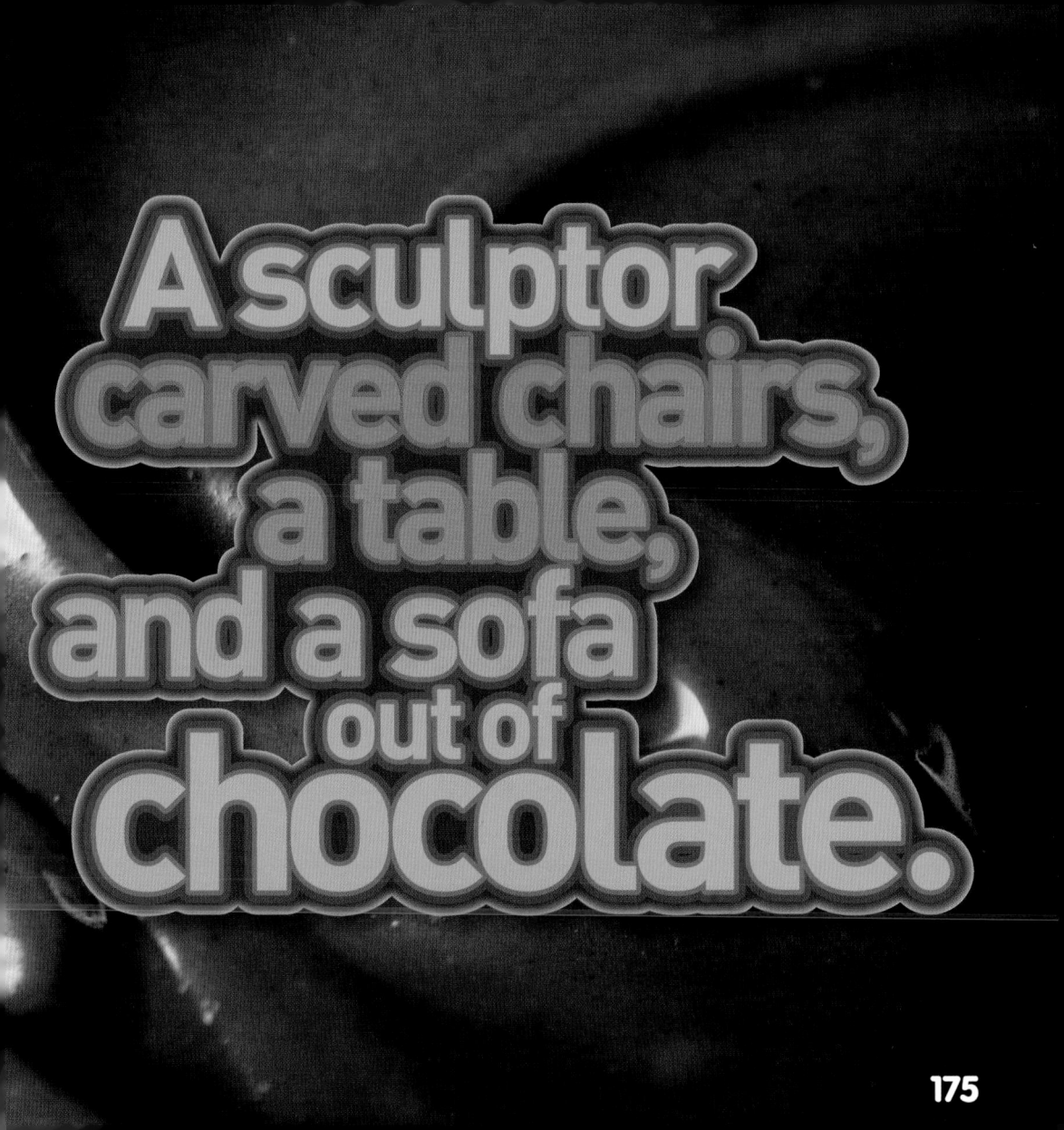
A sculptor carved chairs, a table, and a sofa out of chocolate.

New
York City
Marathon
runners
consume a total of
4,500 pounds
(2,041 kg)
of elbow macaroni
at the annual marathon
eve dinner.

THE 1938 COMIC BOOK
IN WHICH
SUPERMAN
FIRST APPEARED
SOLD FOR
$2.16 MILLION
IN 2011.

SPACE JUNK—
MAN-MADE DEBRIS
FROM SPACE—

FALLS TO EARTH
NEARLY EVERY
WEEK.

Two people separated by ***600 miles*** (966 km) *can see the same* ***shooting star.***

TRAINED OPERA SINGERS CAN REACH NOTES ALMOST AS LOUD AS A JACKHAMMER.

The most popular password on the Internet is "**password.**"

THE PINOCCHIO FROG IS NAMED FOR ITS NOSE THAT CAN INFLATE AND GET POINTIER.

ELEPHANTS
CAN HEAR
EACH OTHER
TRUMPET UP TO
FIVE MILES (8 km)
AWAY.

THERE'S AN ARTIST WHO CREATES TINY PORTRAITS ON

HIS FINGERS.

THE "EVERGLADES PIZZA," SOLD IN A FLORIDA, U.S.A., TOWN, IS TOPPED WITH FROG LEGS, ALLIGATORS, AND PYTHON FILLET!

ONE IN THREE PEOPLE SNEEZE AFTER LOOKING AT THE SUN.

SOME SAUROPOD DINOSAURS' NECKS WERE SIX TIMES LONGER THAN A GIRAFFE'S.

HOT-AIR BALLOONING WAS ONCE AN OLYMPIC SPORT.

A Chinese student designed a postcard that can capture the smell of your favorite food.

THE POPULAR TEXT MESSAGE ABBREVIATION, OMG FOR "OH MY GOD," APPEARED NEARLY 183 YEARS AGO IN A LETTER FROM A BRITISH ADMIRAL.

Early jack-o'-lanterns were carved from turnips, potatoes, and beets.

There are seven quintillion, five hundred quadrillion grains of sand on Earth.

ROBOT JOCKEYS RACE CAMELS IN SAUDI ARABIA.

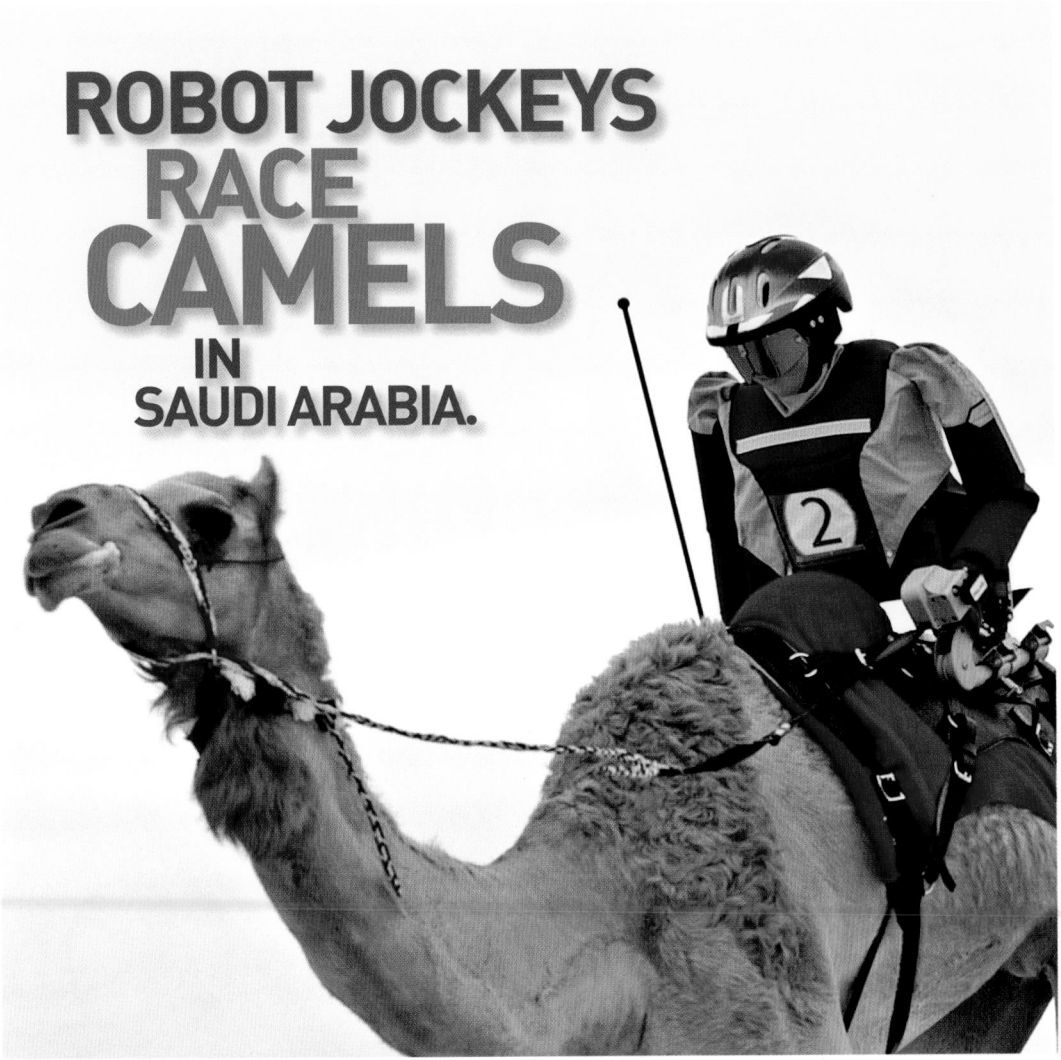

THE WORLD'S TINIEST **GUITAR** IS SMALLER THAN A **SPECK OF DUST.**

IF ALL OF THE **DNA** IN YOUR **BODY** WAS LINED UP, IT COULD **STRETCH** FROM **PLUTO** TO THE **SUN** AND **BACK.**

Google was originally called BackRub.

A man made a **bike** almost entirely out of **cardboard.**

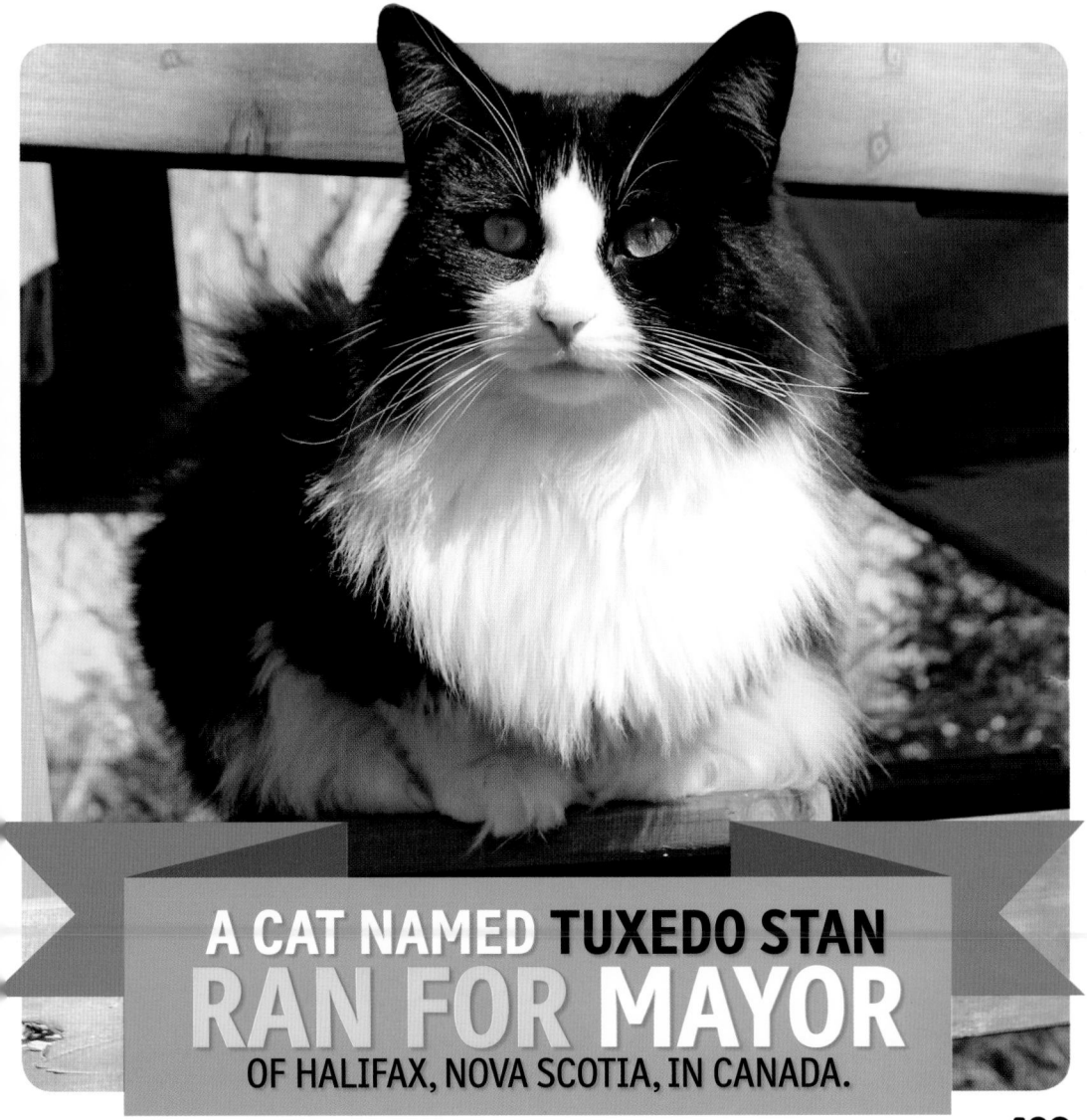

A CAT NAMED **TUXEDO STAN**
RAN FOR MAYOR
OF HALIFAX, NOVA SCOTIA, IN CANADA.

BEES
ONCE MADE
BLUE AND
GREEN
HONEY
AFTER
PICKING UP
COLORFUL
WASTE
FROM AN
M&M'S
FACTORY.

THERE'S ENOUGH ENERGY IN **ONE GALLON** (3.8 L) OF GAS TO CHARGE AN iPHONE FOR 20 YEARS.

A pumpkin has been chucked more than a mile (1.6 km) by a cannon—a world "punkin' chunkin" record!

The planet Uranus was almost named George.

A restaurant filled an aboveground swimming pool with more than 13,780 pounds (6,251 kg) of pasta.

There are more **vending machines in Japan** than there are people in New Zealand.

ONLY 0.1 PERCENT OF BACTERIA ACTUALLY MAKE YOU SICK.

WHALE WASTE IS AN INGREDIENT IN SOME EXPENSIVE PERFUMES.

You're **more sensitive** to **SMELLS** when you're hungry.

CAPTAIN CRUNCH'S FULL NAME IS HORATIO MAGELLAN CRUNCH.

The sky above the **moon** is always black.

A MAN SNOWBOARDED ABOUT 17,500 FEET (5,334 m) DOWN MOUNT EVEREST.

Squirrels **sweat** through their **feet.**

Yuma, Arizona, is the sunniest place in the United States.

Grass looks
greener
to girls than it
does to boys.

28000
UNI

The U.S. President's plane, **Air Force One,** has never landed more than **3 seconds off** its scheduled **arrival time.**

FACTFINDER

Illustrations are indicated by **boldface.**

A

Adults, bad behavior 133, 171
Air Force One (plane) **198–199**, 199
Air pollution 150
Airplanes **28–29**, 29, **198–199**, 199
Albatrosses 151, **151**
Alligators 52–53, **52–53**, 183
Alpacas 162, **162**
Alphabet 85
& ("and" symbol) 85
Angry Birds, inflatable **34–35**, 35
Animal groups **10–11**, 11
Antarctic ice 129, 134
Antarctic icefish 122, **122**
Ants 24, 79, 79, 141, 163, **163**
Aquariums 97
Architecture 45, **45**
Arithmetic **64–65**
Arms 33, 85
Art, on fingers 182, **182**
Assassin bugs 79, **79**
Asteroids 117, **117**
Astraphobia 76–77
Astronauts 121
Atlantic herring **136–137**, 137

B

Babies, taste buds 57
Back, human 33
Bacon 20
Bacteria 193
Bad luck 145
Balloons 74
Bananas 96
Baobab trees 135, **135**
Baseball 51, 140
Basset hounds 90, **90**
Bats 37, 54, **54–55**
Beaches 168
Beagles **106**, 106–107
Beavers 67
Bees 20, 39, **190–191**, 191
Beets 186, **186**
Bell (moose throat flap) 128
Belly buttons, in whales 60, **60**
Ben and Jerry's ice cream 33
Bicycles 72, **72**, 188, **188**
Birds' eggs 68, **68**
Birds' nests 163
Birds' nests soup 103
Blinking 16, 157
Bloat (hippo group) **10–11**, 11
Blood 33, 37, 43, 122
Blue-ringed octopuses **160–161**, 161
Blue whales 24
Blueberries 20, **20**
Board games 115, **115**
Bogles (dog breed) 106–107, **107**
Bone marrow 104
Bonobos 42, **42**
Boring, Oregon, U.S.A. 73
Bowling 80, **80**
Boxers (dog breed) **106**, 106–107
Boys, color vision 197
Brain 69, **69**, 105, 126, 156
Bubble gum 8
Bubblegum coral 158, **158**
Buildings 45, **45**, 75, **75**
Bungee jumping 159, **159**
Buzz Lightyear 88, **88–89**

C

Cairo, Egypt 25, **25**
Camels 25, **25**, 82, **83**, 144, 187, **187**
Captain Crunch 194, **194**
Cardboard bicycle 188, **188**
Cars 14, 120, 144
Cats 154–155, **155**, 189, **189**
Chameleons 78, **78**
Cheeks, taste buds in 57
Cheese, as perfume scent 57, **57**
Chickens 104, 144, **144**

Children's senses 57, 156, 197
Chili peppers 104
China
bad luck 145
birds' nests soup 103
languages 120
pigs 169
postcard smells 186, **186**
Chocolate 31, **31,** 153, 174, **174–175,** 175
Cinespia Theater, California, U.S.A. 152
Clocks 15, **15**
Clothing, from milk powder 18
Cockroaches 73, **73**
Coffee 44, **44**
College students 96
Color vision 197
Comic books 177
Computers 42, **42,** 180
Concentration 98
Corals and coral reefs 158, **158**
Coughing, by fish 67
Cows 61
Crabs **22–23,** 23
Crackers 108
Crickets 85
Crocodiles 105, **105,** 126
Cucumbers 108, **108**

D

Dandelions 134, **134**
Detroit Red Wings 140
Digestion 144
Dinosaurs **4–5,** 5, 30, **30,** 138, **138,** 183, **183**
DNA 188
Doghouses 109, **109**
Dogs 37, **37,** 50, **50, 154,** 154–155
Doodling 98, **98**
Dragonflies **94–95,** 95
Dubai, U.A.E. 75, **75,** 170
Dyes 13

E

Earth (planet) 37, **41,** 119, 140
Eels 84
Eggs 68
Egypt, ancient 62
Eiffel Tower, Paris, France 127, **127**
Elbow macaroni 176, **176**
Elephant seals 148, **148–149**
Elephants 80, 90, 181, **181**
Elvers 84
Energy 47, 192
Energy bars 85, **85**
English alphabet 85
Everest, Mount, China-Nepal 194
"Everglades Pizza" 183
Eyelashes 62, **62**
Eyelids 67, 168
Eyes 20, 103, 138, 156

F

Facebook 150
Falloons 74
Fears 62, 76–77
Ferns 194, **194**
Festivals 142, **142–143**
Finches 92, **92**
Fingernails 122
Fingerprints 55, **55**
Fingers, art on 182, **182**
Finland, islands 21
Fireflies 114, **114**
Fish 67
Fishing nets 26
Flags 168, **168**
Flamingos 164, **164**
Flatworms 138
Football **38**
Footprints 138, **138,** 145, **145**
Forest of crooked trees 172, **172–173**
Four (number), as bad luck 145
Fried bone marrow 104
Frog legs, as pizza topping 183

Frogs 37, **96,** 180, **180**
Furniture, chocolate 175

G

Games, ancient 115, **115**
Garbage 21, **21,** 163
Gasoline 192
Gatorade 7, **7**
Gelada monkeys 164, **164**
Giraffes 12, **12,** 63, **63,** 183
Girls, color vision 197
Glass frogs 86, **86**
Goats 18, 132
Gobblers (male turkeys) 20
Gold, in human body 140
Golden Gate Bridge, San Francisco, California, U.S.A. **70–71,** 71
Golf courses 141
Good luck 66
Google 188
Grass color **196–197,** 197
Graveyards 33, **33,** 152
Green sand beach 168
Grocery stores 146
Guenon monkeys 139, **139**
Guitars 188, **188**
Gummy bears 38, **38**

H

Hair 44, **44,** 50, **50,** 169, 193, **193**
Halifax, Nova Scotia, Canada 189, **189**
Halloween 133, **133,** 186, **186**
Hands, human 157
Havana, Cuba 72, **72**
Hawaii, U.S.A. 168
Hearing 156
Heart 7, 86, **86,** 90
Hello Kitty, on jet **28–29,** 29
Herring **136–137,** 137
Hershey's Kisses 153
Hippopotamuses **10–11,** 11
The Hobbit (movie) 169
Hockey 140
Home runs 140
Homes 150, **150**
Honey 66, **66,** 191
Hornets 129
Horses 18, **18**
Hot-air ballooning **184–185,** 185
Hot dogs 51
Hunger 193
Hurricanes 165

I

Ice 13, 129, 134
Ice cream 19, 33, 92, **92**
Ice hockey 140
Icebergs 112, **112–113**
Injuries 87
Insects 19, 33, 85
International Space Station 88, **88–89**
Internet passwords 180
iPhones 97, 192
iPods 166
Itching 33

J

Jack-o'-lanterns 186, **186**
Jellyfish 69
Jets **28–29,** 29, **198–199,** 199

K

Keyboards 13, **13**
Kinkajous 36, **36**
Komodo dragons 132, **132**

L

Lady Gaga 194
Ladybugs 57
Languages 85, 120, 153

"Lazy Bones" (TV remote) 7
Leapfrog 96
Leeches 43
Lemurs 124, **124, 125**
Lightning 76–77, 84, 164
Lights 103
Lions 91, **91**
Lips 108, **108**
Lollipops 174
Lotteries 84
Luck 66, 145
Lying 171
Lyrebirds 115, **115**

M

Macaroni 176, **176**
Mail 104
Malls 170
Manners 122
Maple syrup 126, **126**
Margarine 80
Mars (planet) 39, **39**
Maya 129
Meat, on *Titanic* 168
Meteor craters 110, **110**
Milk 18, 103
Millipedes 39, 93, **93**
Mississippi River, U.S.A. 165, **165**
M&M's factory 191
Moon 40, **40,** 41, 84, 194, **194**
Moose 128, **128**
Mosquitoes 80
Mountains 117, **117**
Movie theaters 152
Mucus, dye from 13
Mushrooms 62
Mwanza (lizard) 108, **108**

N

NASA traditions 150
Neck size 183, **183**
Nepal, flag 168, **168**
New Year's celebrations 127
New York Marathon 176
Niagara Falls, Canada-U.S.A. 31
Nijo Castle, Japan 51, **51**
Nodding 153
Nosebleeds 20
Noses 141, 180, **180**

O

Ocean
- exploration 41
- sea water 9, 39
- thermal vents 43, **43**
- tubeworms 115, **115**

Octopuses 85, 92, **92,** 140, **160–161,** 161
Olympic Games 116, 185
OMG (abbreviation) 186
Oology 68
Opera singers 180
Orcas 48, **48**
Orchids 109
Ostriches 19
Owls **64**

P

Paint, for structures 71, 127
Parachuting 123, **123**
Parade floats 74
Passwords 180
Pasta 176, **176,** 192
Peacock mantis shrimp 97
Peanuts 150, **150**
Pentecost Island, South Pacific Ocean 159, **159**
Perfume 57, **57,** 193
Piano, from bananas 96
Pigeons 19, **19**
Pigs 67, 169
Pineapples 69, **69**
Ping-pong balls 44, **44**
Pinocchio frogs 180, **180**
Pirate treasure 104

Pizza 56, 163, 183
Platypuses 111, **111**
Poison ivy 18
Police, on camels 25, **25**
Politeness 122
Portraits, on fingers 182, **182**
Postcards 186, **186**
Potato chips 9, **9**
Potatoes 186, **186**
Pound sign 45, **45**
Pumpkins 192
Pythons 183

R

Radishes 138, **138**
Rainbows 109, **109**
Raindrops 27, **27**
Red hair 193, **193**
Red ink 122
Redwood trees 147, **147**
Reindeer 141, **141**
Remote control 7, **7**
Restaurants 192
Rhinoceros beetle 129, **129**
Rhinoceroses 122, **122**
Robots 170, **170,** 187, **187**
Rockets **41**
Roller skating 99, **99**
Romans, ancient 66, 96
Rudeness 122

S

Saliva, in birds' nests 163
Salt, in sea water 9
Saltwater crocodiles 126
Saltwater taffy 39, **39**
Sand 186, **186**
Sauropod dinosaurs 183, **183**
Scratching 33
Sea snails 13
Sea stars 51
Sea water 9, 39
Seattle Space Needle, Washington, U.S.A. **34–35,** 35
Seaweed 67
Seeds, redwood tree 147
Seychelles **100–101,** 101
Sharks 16, **16–17,** 105
Shoes 66, **66,** 127, **127**
Shooting stars 180, **180**
Shopping malls 170
Skateboards 6, **6**
Ski resorts, indoors 170
Skin 7, 86, **86,** 157
Sky color 194, **194**
Sloths 144
Smartphones 103
Smells 121, 156, 186, 193
Snails 13
Snakes 121, 168, 183
Sneakers 127, **127**
Sneezing 183
Snow 92
Snowboarding 194, **194**
Soft drinks 134
Soup 103
Space, smell of 121
Space junk 178–179, **178–179**
Space travel 41, 150
Spaceship Earth, Walt Disney World Resort, Florida, U.S.A. **58–59,** 59
Spiders 26, **26,** 62, 105
Squirrels 195, **195**
Stomachs 51, 157
Strawberries 145, **145**
Strikes (bowling) 80
Sun 39, **39,** 102, **102,** 183, 196
Sunfish **130–131,** 131
Superman 177, **177**
Sweating 108, 195
Swiflets 163, **163**
Swimming 19, 111, **111**
Swimming pools 192

T

T. rex **4–5,** 5
Tabasco sauce 39, **39**
Tapeworms 168
Tarantulas 49, **49**
Taste buds 57, 154–155, 157
"Tater" (home run) 140
Taxes 66
Teeth 30, 52–53, **52–53,** 67
Television remotes 7, **7**
Text messages 186
Thermal vents 43, **43**
Thunder, fear of 76–77
Titanic, R.M.S. 168
Titanoboas 121
Todaiji Temple, Japan 110, **110**
Toilets 7, 32, **32,** 129
Tongue 78, **78**
Toothbrushes 67
Tornadoes **46–47,** 47, 110
Tortoises **100–101,** 101
Touch receptors 157
Trees, crooked 172, **172–173**
Triceratops 30, **30**
Tubeworms 115, **115**
Tuna 163
Turkey (bowling feat) 80
Turkeys (bird) 20
Turnips 186, **186**
Turtles 43, **43, 100–101,** 101
Tut, King (Egypt) 115
Tuxedo Stan (cat) 189, **189**
Twitter 73, 127
2001 (movie) 166, **166–167**
Typewriter (word) 13

U

Uranus (planet) 192

V

Vampire bats 37
Vending machines 12, **12,** 193
Venus (planet) 56
Vesta (asteroid) 117, **117**
Vision 156, 197
Volcanoes 56

W

Wagons 81, **81**
Wallabies 126
Walt Disney World Resort, Florida, U.S.A. **58–59,** 59
Wars 19, 129, 153
Water 13, 80
Water fights 127
Waterfalls 31
Weddings 37, **37,** 66
Weight 37, 121, 124, 131
Whales 24, 60, **60,** 80, 193
White orcas 48, **48**
Wigs 50, **50,** 169
Wildflowers 31, **31**
Windshield wipers 14
Winter, full moon 40
Woodpeckers 153, **153**
World War II 153

Y

Yaks **168–169,** 169
Yawning 147
Yosemite National Park, California, U.S.A. 109, **109**
Yuma, Arizona, U.S.A. 196

CELEBRATING 125 YEARS

The National Geographic Society is one of the world's largest nonprofit scientific and educational organizations. Founded in 1888 to "increase and diffuse geographic knowledge," the Society's mission is to inspire people to care about the planet. It reaches more than 400 million people worldwide each month through its official journal, *National Geographic*, and other magazines; National Geographic Channel; television documentaries; music; radio; films; books; DVDs; maps; exhibitions; live events; school publishing programs; interactive media; and merchandise. National Geographic has funded more than 10,000 scientific research, conservation, and exploration projects and supports an education program promoting geographic literacy.

For more information, please call
1-800-NGS LINE (647-5463) or
write to the following address:
National Geographic Society
1145 17th Street N.W.
Washington, D.C. 20036-4688 U.S.A.

Visit us online at nationalgeographic.com/books

For librarians and teachers: ngchildrensbooks.org

More for kids from National Geographic:
kids.nationalgeographic.com

For information about special discounts for bulk purchases, please contact National Geographic Books Special Sales: ngspecsales@ngs.org

For rights or permissions inquiries, please contact National Geographic Books Subsidiary Rights: ngbookrights@ngs.org

Published by the National Geographic Society
John M. Fahey, *Chairman of the Board and Chief Executive Officer*
Timothy T. Kelly, *President*
Declan Moore, *Executive Vice President; President, Publishing and Travel*
Melina Gerosa Bellows, *Executive Vice President; Chief Creative Officer, Books, Kids, and Family*

Prepared by the Book Division
Hector Sierra, *Senior Vice President and General Manager*
Nancy Laties Feresten, *Senior Vice President, Kids Publishing and Media*
Jonathan Halling, *Design Director, Books and Children's Publishing*
Jay Sumner, *Director of Photography, Children's Publishing*
Jennifer Emmett, *Vice President, Editorial Director, Children's Books*
R. Gary Colbert, *Production Director*
Jennifer A. Thornton, *Director of Managing Editorial*

Staff for This Book
Robin Terry, *Project Manager*
Sarah Wassner Flynn, *Project Editor*
Eva Absher, *Art Director*
Rachael Hamm Plett, *Designer*
Callie Broaddus, *Design Production Assistant*
Julie Beer, Michelle Harris, *Researchers*
Ariane Szu-Tu, *Editorial Assistant*
Hillary Moloney, *Illustrations Editor*
Grace Hill, Michael O'Connor, *Associate Managing Editors*
Joan Gossett, *Production Editor*
Lewis R. Bassford, *Production Manager*
Susan Borke, *Legal and Business Affairs*

Based on the "Weird But True" department in *National Geographic Kids* magazine

Manufacturing and Quality Management
Phillip L. Schlosser, *Senior Vice President*
Chris Brown, *Vice President, NG Book Manufacturing*
George Bounelis, *Vice President, Production Services*
Rachel Faulise, *Manager*
Nicole Elliott, *Manager*
Robert Barr, *Manager*

***WEIRD BUT TRUE 5!* PHOTO CREDITS**

ALL ARTWORK BY RACHAEL HAMM PLETT UNLESS OTHERWISE NOTED BELOW:

COVER, KENT KOBERSTEEN/NATIONAL GEOGRAPHIC STOCK; 2, KENT KOBERSTEEN/NATIONAL GEOGRAPHIC STOCK; 4-5, FRANCO TEMPESTA; 6, CALIFORNIA SKATEPARKS/SOLENT NEWS ; 9, ALEXANDR MAKAROV/SHUTTERSTOCK; 9, FOTOMAK/SHUTTERSTOCK; 10-11, FRANS LANTING/NATIONAL GEOGRAPHIC STOCK; 16-17, CBPIX CBPIX/ISTOCKPHOTO; 18, AUSTIN HARGRAVE; 20, BRIGGS PLANT PROPAGATORS; 22-23, DR. HENDRIK FREITAG/DEPARTMENT OF BIOLOGICAL SCIENCES, NATIONAL UNIVERSITY OF SINGAPORE: THE RAFFLES BULLETIN OF ZOOLOGY 60: PP.37-55; 25, JACK SULLIVAN/ALAMY; 26, RA-PHOTOS/ISTOCKPHOTO; 27, JACKISO/SHUTTERSTOCK; 28-29, KYODO/REUTERS; 30, FRANCO TEMPESTA; 32, GREG WOOD/AFP/GETTY IMAGES; 34-35, GOODNIGHT RED BALLOON; 36, CLAUDIO CONTRERAS/NPL/MINDEN PICTURES; 38, PCN PHOTOGRAPH/ALAMY; 38, KELLEY TIBBLE/DREAMSTIME.COM; 38, WESTEND61 GMBH/ALAMY; 39, NASA; 40-41, MARILYN BARBONE/SHUTTERSTOCK; 41, NASA; 42, LIZ RUPERT PUGH; 43, WIKIPEDIA/NOAA; 44, RACHAEL HAMM-PLETT; 45, BIG-BJARKE INGELS GROUP; 46-47, FRANKLIN REYES; 75 (LE), ADAM REED TUCKER/LEGO/EXPRESS02222/FLICKR; 75 (RT), FRANCESCO DAZZI/SHUTTERSTOCK; 78, CATHY KEIFER/SHUTTERSTOCK; 79, KURT_G/SHUTTERSTOCK; 81, MMX STEVEN E. GROSS; 83, DAVID EVISON/ISTOCKPHOTO; 86, JOEL SARTORE/NATIONAL GEOGRAPHIC STOCK; 88-89, NASA; 89 (UP), PICTAFOLIO/ISTOCKPHOTO; 90, ERIC ISSELEE/SHUTTERSTOCK; 91, REDMICH/ISTOCKPHOTO; 92 (LE), WIKIPEDIA; 92 (RT), TRATONG/SHUTTERSTOCK; 93, ANDREW RICHARDS/BOHART MUSEUM; 94, CATHY KEIFER/SHUTTERSTOCK; 96, ASHWAY/ALAMY; 98, REBECCA HALE, NGP; 98, JOSHLAVERTY/ISTOCKPHOTO; 99, BETTMANN/CORBIS; 100-101, PETE OXFORD/NATUREPL.COM; 104, NORTH WIND PICTURE ARCHIVES/ALAMY; 106, ERIK LAM/SHUTTERSTOCK; 106, GLOBALP/ISTOCKPHOTO; 107, JOHNNYMAD/ISTOCKPHOTO; 108, SUBJUG/ISTOCKPHOTO; 108, BERND ROHRSCHNEIDER/MINDEN PICTURES; 109, JONSON/DREAMSTIME.COM; 109, LA PETITE MAISON; 110, EARTH SCIENCES AND IMAGE ANALYSIS LABORATORY, NASA JOHNSON SPACE CENTER; 110, SEAN PAVONE/DREAMSTIME.COM; 111, DAVE WATTS/ALAMY; 112-113, RALPH LEE HOPKINS/NATIONAL GEOGRAPHIC STOCK; 115 (UP), CULTNAT, DIST. RMN-GP/ART RESOURCE, NY; 115 (LO), WIKIPEDIA; 117, WIKIPEDIA; 118-119, SANDRO L. RAMOS/SHUTTERSTOCK; 120, EXACTOSTOCK/SUPERSTOCK; 120, JANKS/DREAMSTIME.COM; 122, JASON PRINCE/SHUTTERSTOCK; 122, FLIP NICKLEN/MINDEN PICTURES; 123, U.S. AIR FORCE; 124, MARK THIESSEN, NGS; 125, ARTO HAKOLA/SHUTTERSTOCK; 126, D. HURST/ALAMY; 127, NASH MONEY/DESIGNBOOM; 128, ARNOLD JOHN LABRENTZ/SHUTTERSTOCK; 129, ARLIND071/ISTOCKPHOTO; 130-131, DANIEL BOTELHO/BARCROFT MEDIA LTD./LANDOV MEDIA; 132, JAKGREE/DREAMSTIME.COM; 133, TRAVELER1116/ISTOCKPHOTO; 134, IROCHKA/DREAMSTIME.COM; 135, WIKIPEDIA; 136-137, FRANCO BANFI/WATERFRAME RM/GETTY IMAGES; 138, WIKIPEDIA; 138, FRANCESG29/FLICKR; 139, WORLDSWILDLIFEWONDERS/SHUTTERSTOCK; 142-143, ALBERT GEA/REUTERS; 144, WILLEECOLE/SHUTTERSTOCK; 145, ALASDAIRJAMES/ISTOCKPHOTO; 147, JFTRINGALI/ISTOCKPHOTO; 148-149, JOHN EASCOTT AND WA MOMTIUK/NATIONAL GEOGRAPHIC STOCK; 151, IAKOV KALININ/SHUTTERSTOCK; 153, GERALD MARELLA/SHUTTERSTOCK; 154, GLOBALP/ISTOCKPHOTO; 155, DRBIMAGES/ISTOCKPHOTO; 156-157, DEREK LATTA/ISTOCKPHOTO; 158, COURTESY OF THE MONTEREY BAY AQUARIUM RESEARCH INSTITUTE (C) 2006 MBARI; 159, ADAM&TONI/FLICKR; 160-161, RICHARD MERRITT FRPS/GETTY IMAGES; 162, JUNIORS BILDARCHIV GMBH/ALAMY; 163, YINGXIAOMING/ISTOCKPHOTO; 164, GUENTERGUNI/ISTOCKPHOTO; 165, RIGOULET GILLES/SUPERSTOCK; 166-167, SUNSET BOULEVARD/CORBIS; 167, DRFELICE/SHUTTERSTOCK; 168, MICROSTOCK MAN/SHUTTERSTOCK; 169, ERIC ISSELEE/SHUTTERSTOCK; 170, THOMAS VOGEL/SHUTTERSTOCK; 171, THOMAS NORTHCUT/SUPERSTOCK; 172-173, SEAWHISPER/SHUTTERSTOCK; 174-175, SUBBOTINA ANNA/SHUTTERSTOCK; 176, FRANK L JUNIOR/SHUTTERSTOCK; 178-179, NASA; 180, TIM LAMAN/NATIONAL GEOGRAPHIC STOCK; 181, EDSTOCK/ISTOCKPHOTO; 182 (UPLE), DITO VON TESSE; 182 (UP CTR), DITO VON TESE; 182 (UPRT), DITO VON TESE; 182 (LOLE), DITO VON TESE; 182 (LOCTR), DITO VON TESE; 182 (LORT), DITO VON TESE; 183, FRANCO TEMPESTA; 184-185, SJLAYNE/ISTOCKPHOTO; 186, LUCENTIUS/ISTOCKPHOTO; 186, BURIY/ISTOCKPHOTO; 186, DEVONYU/ISTOCKPHOTO; 187, AP IMAGES/KAMRAN JEBREILI; 188, COURTESY OF HAROLD CRAIGHEAD, CORNELL UNIVERSITY; 188, PAPER PIRATE CO.; 188, KRIANGKRAI WANGJAI/SHUTTERSTOCK; 189, HUGH CHISHOLM; 190-191, VINCENT KESSLER/REUTERS; 192, ITHINKSKY/ISTOCKPHOTO; 193, LINDAYOLANDA/ISTOCKPHOTO; 194, ARTENS/SHUTTERSTOCK; 195, PATRIK MEZIRKA/SHUTTERSTOCK; 196-197, JANNOON028/SHUTTERSTOCK; 196, CAMMERAYDAVE/DREAMSTIME.COM; 196, MARILYN GOULD/DREAMSTIME.COM; 198-199, U.S. AIR FORCE.

NATIONAL GEOGRAPHIC KIDS ALMANAC!

The ultimate all-in-one FUN-TASTIC fact-finding homework-helping boredom-busting book!

Available wherever books are sold.

Want more?

These books are PACKED with extraordinary FUN-tastic facts for the SUPER SENSATIONAL YOU!

AVAILABLE WHEREVER BOOKS ARE SOLD

Find us at Facebook.com/NatGeoBooks